Vertical Gardens

Vertical Gardens

LEIGH CLAPP & HATTIE KLOTZ

NH
NEW HOLLAND

CONTENTS

INTRODUCTION

With this book we hope to inspire you to look up next time you are out walking in the city, or out working in your garden. Gardens that stretch into the sky are a growing feature of urban living, covering hard concrete surfaces with lush, lovely greenery. As our lives become more crowded and our disconnection from nature more profound, there's so much potential to garden in new ways, using the vertical plane.

This book offers inspiration from some of the most creative minds working in landscape design. It also offers some simple ideas for you to try in your own garden at home. It explains the various systems available for creating green walls and offers practical advice on which plants work where. It will show you how to create an edible garden when you think you just don't have space – you do! – and it will fill you with easy, more traditional ideas to add vertical elements to your garden.

Garden on, garden up!

Chapter 1

IN HISTORY

The world's first vertical garden may not even have existed. While scientists and archeologists, historians, classicists and botanists can't decide where, or even when the Hanging Gardens of Babylon might have been, expert opinion appears to be centering on Nineveh in northern Iraq, the garden inspired the imagination of a legion of ancient writers.

The mere awe-inspiring idea of gardens reaching far into the sky landed the Hanging Gardens on the list of the Seven Ancient Wonders of the World.

Nowadays, gardens towering several hundreds of feet into the air are a reality and becoming increasingly common. From the 150-metre tall Central Park Tower in Sydney, swathed in over 38,000 plants, to smaller scale residential projects in urban settings, both indoors and outdoors worldwide, gardening is no longer confined to the ground. Landscape designers are looking up for inspiration and a new canvas.

It all began in the early part of the 20th century. Stanley Hart White was a professor of Landscape Architecture at the University of Illinois from 1922 until 1959. While his name is not widely known in the world of vertical gardening, he is considered to be the inventor of the first vertical gardening system since he filed a patent for his invention of "Botanical Bricks" in 1937. However, his brick system never went into commercial production and his name remains obscure.

However his French namesake, Patrick Blanc, is widely credited with bringing the first vertical gardens into commercial production. Blanc, a botanist, scientist and artist is a modern innovator, fascinated by plants that grow on rock faces, trees and overhanging cliffs in the wild. He has invented a soilless system to grow plants on vertical surfaces based on non-biodegradable artificial felt. He has completed over 250 projects worldwide since his first in 1986 in Paris at the Cité des Sciences et de l'Industrie la Villette.

While Blanc may have literally sowed the seeds to create gardens in the sky, he has created a roadmap with plants for others to follow in his footsteps. There are numerous systems now available commercially that allow professionals and amateurs alike to cultivate vertical gardens.

FROM COMMERCIAL TO RESIDENTIAL

As the technical requirements for green wall vertical gardening have become less daunting with the invention of relatively simple automated feeding and watering systems, green walls and vertical gardens have passed from the purely commercial – municipal buildings, universities, offices, hotels, museums, apartment buildings and store fronts – to the residential.

What is most important when considering any project, is scale. The larger the space to be covered, the more likely you are to need professional help, especially in the planning and planting stages. Even a small space can demand hundreds, sometimes thousands of plants. Density is an important consideration, as a patchy project punctuated by gaps looks immediately scruffy and won't achieve the desired effect of building a three dimensional tapestry wall made of leaves, texture and colour.

WHY CREATE A VERTICAL GARDEN?

It's no secret that the world is becoming increasingly urbanised. Mass migration from a rural to an urban lifestyle has taken place during the past 150 years.

In 2008, for the first time in history, more than half the world's population lived in cities. If the trend continues at the same pace, more than 70 per cent of us will live in urban environments by 2050. Even in the greenest of cities, this represents a severe disconnection with nature.

It's also no secret that contact with nature has positive mental health benefits. Who can deny that a couple of hours spent walking in the countryside or digging in the dirt makes you feel happy? Numerous academic studies have found that, "the balance of evidence indicates conclusively that knowing and experiencing nature makes us generally happier, healthier people."* Just the proximity of plants and trees makes our air cleaner and our moods brighter. Vertical gardening is just one more way to make our cities greener and reclaim unused urban space that might otherwise remain barren, reclaiming concrete landscapes to give them a softer edge and put them to use to improve the air we breathe.

Green infrastructure has been shown to improve air quality substantially. A recent study at the University of Lancaster in the UK and Karlsruhe Institute of Technology in Germany has shown that green living walls can have a big impact on levels of nitrogen dioxide and particulate matter in urban street canyons (those tunnel-like spaces between tall buildings), reducing levels by up to 40 per cent and 60 per cent respectively.

In places where even the smallest parcel of land is worth more than the annual salary of a worker on minimum wage – Manhattan, Hong Kong, Central London – where $1-million buys just 20 square metres of property on average, the only feasible way to garden is up.

In London's Mayfair neighbourhood, The Athenaeum Hotel decided to do exactly that. Found close to Hyde Park corner on Piccadilly, on a highly visible corner, the art deco hotel is swathed from sidewalk to sky, eight storeys high in vibrant green. Patrick Blanc completed the project in 2009, using over 260 species and 12,000 individual plants to cover the façade, mirroring Green Park on the opposite side of the road. Offering an important haven for insects and birds, it's also a fun surprise when you're riding a red bus towards the hustle and bustle of Piccadilly Circus.

There's something whimsical, Dr. Suess-esque about plants waving wildly from walls and the sides of buildings. But while they might be fun and seem frivolous, vertical gardens can offer important ecological benefits. They can offer a safe place to land and to feed for a myriad of insects and birds. They can house bee hotels and aid in urban pollination and biodiversity. They offer substantial noise reduction properties, helping to absorb the clatter and clang of city life. They also contribute a cooling effect to the urban environment working to mitigate the effect of building heating and cooling systems, cars, people, buses and trains that cause noise and heat islands, a symptom of modern living in concrete and asphalt cities. On the other hand, in winter they offer substantial insulating benefits. This, in turn, offers reductions in energy consumption.

Green walls can also help with water management issues. Like their cousins green roofs, green walls can help absorb water after heavy rainstorms. It's a simple equation: increased green infrastructure offers more potential for reducing storm water runoff.

While this might seem counter-intuitive, green walls can actually help to protect buildings from degradation. Not only do they mitigate the impact of direct sunlight, but by offering insulating properties, they help reduce the expansion and contraction caused by extremes of temperature.

Chapter 2

IN DESIGN

As interior designers are increasingly looking to the fifth wall in houses – the ceiling – so too, gardeners and garden designers are looking to the vertical plane in gardens. There's no reason why a garden must be horizontal. In fact, varying the planes and heights in your garden adds as much interest as a good variety of plants.

Using vertical surfaces is a chance to create a green cocoon, feathering hard vertical planes with plants, much as you would any regular garden bed. It is important to think of your vertical garden as you would your regular garden – it's simply another surface to incorporate into your outdoor living plan.

HEATHER GARDEN

A feature wall is a great way to showcase a particular plant. In this case, thirty-six varieties of heather steal the spotlight, planted both in the wall and flowerbeds.

Designed by William Quarmby for a modern, urban family, looking for a low maintenance garden, it was arranged over three levels, including a small water element and a place for outdoor dining. This is a large garden – stretching to 60 square metres – but can easily be scaled down for smaller spaces.

The feature, boundary wall at the back is a living wall, grown from a patchwork of heathers, arranged in a checkerboard pattern. It was built using the gravity fed Vertigarden soil system, and ties the heather in the vertical wall to the heathers used in the horizontal garden. The wall produces white, pink and violet flowers during the winter and spring, while the heathers planted in the flowerbeds produce colour in summer and autumn, offering a moving, changing palette.

Heathers are a great choice because they're hardy, easy to maintain and are very attractive to pollinators, year round. To capitalise on this, Quarmby chose to host a live bumblebee colony in the garden and incorporated a lodge into the design.

He included ferns, grasses, a few shade plants and a limited selection of perennials, with an eye on keeping annual maintenance to a minimum. To keep the living wall in tiptop condition, it needs annual trimming after flowering and a liquid feed added to the automatic watering system as needed.

Hard landscaping elements include a dry stonewall which stretches the length of the living wall, sandstone on the ground and timber cladding, both of which offer natural contrast with the lush greenery.

BUDDHA GARDEN

At just 18 square metres, this urban garden shows the potential for a small space. It integrates a lush living wall into a tropical design scheme. Featuring a golden Buddha, a pair of tree ferns, a stone bench and a water feature with small fountains in the middle of the rill, it offers a green cocoon from the surrounding built environment and city noise.

Designed by Philip Nixon and installed using a soil-based system from ANS Global, the garden was installed and is maintained by Scotscape. The system relies on a simple watering system from a tap on a timer that drains to a gutter at the foot of the wall. To keep it in top shape, the wall requires twice monthly pruning, feeding – which is done using a hand sprayer - and checking for pests and disease.

The wall is now several years old, so pruning is important to stop the plants from overshadowing one another and to maintain the tropical vibe without it turning to rain forest abundance.

MONACO GARDEN

For a Mediterranean feel or location, more drought tolerant planting can be used in living walls, such as lampranthus and osteospermum. With outdoor living year round, the garden with its green walls becomes another room of the house and must tie in with cohesive design, from garden furniture to the hard landscaping elements.

Here, designer Sarah Eberle has created an urban green space designed to reduce energy consumption used for heating and cooling. Inspired by the principality of Monaco, which has pledged to devote 20 per cent of all new development to green space, Eberle focuses on the very small green spaces found in the country. She makes the most of every plane to give the feeling of being surrounded by nature. The 220 square metre garden included two green walls, grown using the Biotecture hydroponic system, the inspiration for which was the hanging Jardin Exotique, which flows down the rock face as one enters Monaco.

A cantilevered roof is planted with lavender, which offers the soft, purple glow so reminiscent of the South of France when flowering. It's a colour that Eberle chose to pick up in the daybeds and painted concrete flowerbed retaining walls elsewhere in the garden. All the timber used in the project was eucalyptus, for a sustainable solution, while the stone is similar to that found in the South of France.

CONTEMPORARY COURTYARD GARDEN

It's possible for a garden to be green by every interpretation of the word. This 35 square metre garden designed by Kate Gould turned an unused urban space between buildings into a green retreat for members of the public.

Not only did she incorporate a living wall, but hard landscaping elements are also made largely from sustainable, permeable and recycled materials. Walls are built from breezeblocks, faced in Portland stone. While the ground surface is a fully permeable CEDEC, which is natural gravel hoggin.

Designed in crisp white and green, juxtaposed with the golden hue of cedar wood accents, the garden offers an oasis of green from windows above, and also a place of respite from city noise below, cocooned in green. The absorbent nature of the living wall, planted using an ANS Global soil-based system, flowerbeds and permeable surfaces also helps with the issues of water run-off in an urban environment during heavy rain.

COURTYARD PANEL

This small courtyard living wall panel is a departure from the majority of green wall design schemes. Most tend to be very structured with planting plans that lead towards the graphic, giving a tapestry effect. This living wall, grown using a hydroponic system by Biotecture, offers a loose, wild feeling, as if the plants have made their own home, growing up the wall.

The panel reflects the feeling found elsewhere in the space, of a wild, abundant cottage garden, featuring woodland plants such as foxglove, ferns and soft grasses. The designers also choose to represent the therapeutic link between gardens and wellbeing, featuring medicinal, aromatic and sensory plants in relaxing tones of purple, blue and white. It is 42 square metres, the size of a small town garden.

Inorganic elements in this 42 square metre garden (size of a small town garden) include a round Darley Moore Yorkstone terrace, curved oak bench and slatted softwood walls.

WHITE COURTYARD

A simple palette of white, green and wood, defines this contemporary courtyard at the rear of an urban home. Designed by Belderbos Landscapes, the living walls were installed by Mark Laurence, using the Vertology system, and act as a green screen between neighbours, offering a haven for wildlife. The garden is approximately 70 square metres and features three vertical walls, along with clean-lined wood accents in the form of a bench, slatted fence and underfoot decking.

The main wall, which features a stainless steel water feature at the centre, is offset from the other two, offering a place to hide the mechanics of the set-up behind it. The wall is automatically watered and fertilised during the growing season and requires pruning two to three times annually. The nutrient dosing is turned off during the winter.

The green garden cocoon offers an outdoor entertaining retreat as well as serenity, privacy and calm in a simple, three colour palette of green, white and wood with the soothing sound of running water in the background.

FERN OASIS GARDEN
In this contemporary garden space, vertical elements are front and centre.

Designer Matthew Childs chose to include an 18 square metre lush fern-filled living wall including Polypodium, Dryopteris and Athyrium, as well as a line of pleached *Liquidambar styraciflua* 'Worplesdon' trees that he sourced in Belgium. The trees allow an element of transparency and light, yet still provide adequate screening.

The wall, installed using the soil-based Easiwall by Treebox planting system, and pleached trees give a strong sense of a green cocoon, focusing one's attention inwards on the contemporary cedar pergola columns, seating and decking, stone work, copper accents and running water. The living wall was in part shade at the back of the garden - so plants were chosen to create a lush fern wall. The wall was the backdrop to a pergola area with seating, surrounded by water. "I wanted to achieve a tranquil effect. It was important that this area felt enclosed and intimate and the green wall created this sense of enclosure. Its textural, green nature softened the space and made it feel much more inviting than, say, a wall," explains Childs.

OUTDOOR ROOM

This rectilinear design for an Australian-Malaysian couple was envisioned to capture the lush, green tropical spaces of their home countries, provide an extension of the contemporary living space with an indoor-outdoor space for entertaining and a play area for the couple's young son.

The 1.8-metre tall walls and the extending finger walls were planted using the Scotscape fabric pocket semi-hydroponic soil-based system. Designer Arit Andersen also included a slate water feature wall, lit from the pebble-filled water reservoir below, and used the walls to create interest, keeping the horizontal 40-plus square metre space clear for the serious business of playing.

Hand made solid oak benches sit on a framework clad with black riven slate tiles, while a pergola provides a sense of enclosure. Copper rain chains provide conduits for water runoff, in place of downpipes. The owners chose artificial grass because it's dirt-free, permeable and doesn't require watering, but also because the house has ground source heating, which meant no paving nor large trees or shrubs.

WATER FEATURES AND LIVING WALLS

Where there are plants, there must be water. It's not a huge leap to add a water feature to your vertical garden or living wall and it adds a whole extra level of sensory stimulation; the soothing sound of falling water to block out city noise and the silvery energy of moving water.

This contemporary metal planter with three spouts offers the perfect contrast to the small leaved, silvery planting scheme on the wall above. Plants here include tiarella, viola, begonia and bergenia. Easily incorporated into smaller spaces, this water feature would work well in a contemporary urban garden.

The rusted Corten steel waterfall contrasts nicely with the lush, slightly wild and wet wall to either side. At 1.9-metres tall, it really gives the feeling of a jungle landscape, while the dark spines of the ferns and the underside of the giant *Rheum palmatum* leaves pick up the rusted tones of the water feature.

Designed by Patrick Collins, using the Biotecture hydroponic system, the garden represents the journey of babies and their parents after a difficult birth: a turbulent start (represented by the waterfall) ending in a calmer place, further downstream.

WATERFALLS

Far more ambitious is a large waterfall feature such as the one found in The Hidden Beauty of Kranji - Singapore Garden.

Built to replicate a live cliff face, a three-tiered waterfall cascades over the green living wall, built using the Uniseal system, offering the soothing sounds of falling water. The inspiration for this tropical paradise was Kranji, a suburb of Singapore, a city known for limited green space. This garden showed the potential for creating a lush tropical paradise in a city garden. Featuring a living seating area cascading with climbing plants and a green roof garden containing a circular glass, water-filled window, it included tropical orchids, palm and fig trees for further vertical elements.

Inspiration for this compact city garden came from Japan, with design by Fuminari Todaka. Designed with families and children in mind, the space creates a green cocoon, shielded from ambient urban noise by a pair of green walls. Soft surfaces abound, including a raised green bench that could even be used as a bed, and green handrails. But the focus of this private space is the cascading, shower-like waterfall, suspended between the green walls.

Todaka planted the vertical elements using a soil-based system, with plastic cassette-type plant holders imported from Japan. The walls were watered with an automatic system and measured approximately 48 square feet each.

While the shower offers the perfect place for children to play, for adults who don't want to get wet, the soothing sounds of constantly moving water offer a moment of respite from urban noise.

Chapter 3

TO CAMOUFLAGE — WALLS, GATES AND BOUNDARIES

That garden wall that you share with your neighbour is an excellent canvas for unlimited creativity. Walls and fences offer an opportunity to expand your garden to create living walls, and to incorporate those new garden spaces into your outdoor living plan.

Often, they're also ugly. So you'll be making a couple of birds and plenty of insects happy if you treat your garden walls, gates and boundaries as an extension of your gardening space. Who wants to look at tired brick or crumbling concrete anyway?

While the initial infrastructure for camouflaging these vertical planes might be a little more complex than bunging a tree or shrub into the ground to hide an unsightly downpipe or other building feature, the extra set-up is worth the effort for the cocooning green beauty that results. With built-in irrigation systems, once a green wall is set up, it will help purify your garden air, offer a sense of green cocooning and it'll certainly become a talking point.

BIRD BOX WALL

Installed on an existing brick garden wall, this green wall planted with ferns *Asplenium trichomanes*, *Asplenium scolopendrium* and *Blechnum spicant*, covers just over 14 square metres. Grown in a soil-based system (mostly compost with horticultural grit) of fabric hanging pockets, the wall was installed on a powder coated metal frame that was screwed into the wall, which allows any excess water to drain, means that the panels do not sit directly against the wall and gives a clean finish. It also provides an insulating layer to the exterior.

The wall needs mains water supply and a drainage channel, and is irrigated using a small pump. There's very little excess water as the wall is managed so that just the right amount of moisture is delivered to the plants. A separate fertiliser tank and irrigation line is needed, but the mechanics of this can be hidden elsewhere in the garden. The wall needs fortnightly maintenance during the summer and monthly attention during the winter. About 10 to 30 plants need to be replaced annually.

Green walls are already a haven for insects, but the client requested that the designer, Cameron Landscapes and Gardens, also add the bird boxes to encourage feathered friends.

CONTEMPORARY ENTRANCE

A modern urban street scene shows what can be achieved in even the smallest space. Designed by Ian Dexter, it was planted using the US made ELT system, which grows plants in a peat-free compost medium. Two thick and vibrant green walls flank a simple pathway, in stark contrast to the minimalist front door and the ultra-low planting to the right. (See image at the right)

STONE AND GREEN WALL

This camouflage green wall was grown around vertical granite slabs, using the hydroponic Vertology Plantbrick™ system, which allows plants to grow in the smallest spaces. Designed by LDC Gardens to stimulate all the senses through a series of contrasting sensory experiences for the blind, partially blind and sighted, the green wall featured soft plants such as *Soleirolia soleirolii*, *Polystichum aculeatum*, *Pachysandra terminalis*, *Hosta* 'Halcyon' and *Hedera helix* 'Wonder', moss and ferns to contrast with the hard granite accents. The Plantbrick™ vertical system allowed the designers to work around the natural rock elements, even adding trickling water to the wall. (See image at the left)

MIXED PLANTING

This bold and very full green wall was an example of what can be achieved from Scotscape. Planted in their own light-weight semi-hydroponic modular panel system constructed from a patented advanced geotextile fabric, the demonstration wall included *Heuchera* 'marble', basil, thyme, sage, *Pachysandra terminalis*, and hosta. Each square metre length of textile holds 49 plants in individual pockets and is irrigated and fed by a drip line.
(See image at the right)

BEACH HOUSE

Typically, gardening close to the ocean requires a special approach because of the nature of the environment with strong winds and salty water and air. Here, a beach house incorporates a low green wall into the architectural design of the building. Stretching around two sides of the house, which faces an estuary, this foundation green wall was installed using the soil-based system from ANS Global.

Plants were carefully chosen to be hardy for wind, salt and weather and include *Euonymus*, *Erysimum* 'Bowles's Mauve' and *Lamium* 'beacon silver'. (See images at the right and below)

GATE

A green wall approach can even be used to hide an ugly gate. In these pictures, the Scotscape modular semi-hydroponic panel system, which is light enough not to overweight the gate, was used to grow an abundant mixture of annuals and perennials, including *Skimmia japonica* 'Rubella', *Viola* tri-colour, *Erigeron karvinskianus*, *Polypodium vulgare*, *Bergenia cordifolia*, *Luzula nivea* and *sylvatica*, and *Pelargonium pelatum*. (See image at the left)

INSECT HOTEL

One of the benefits of green walls is their appeal to insects: butterflies, insects and bees are always happy to find additional sources of food and places to rest. The installation of an insect hotel takes this one step further. Not only is there a safe place to rest among the holes and crevices of the drilled out logs and within the wooden frame, but also an abundant source of food is right next door. An insects' paradise!

Imogen Cox designed the insect hotel and living wall using the Vertiflora soil-based system. It features ferns and edible plants.

INSECT HOUSE

In this trial wall for insects, designers at Scotscape inserted a small house into a green wall, making sure to choose plants that were especially appealing to insects such as lupins, poppies and thistles.

DIVIDING WALL

If you love your neighbour, but not so much that you want to see him over the garden wall, one solution is to green that wall, giving it volume and height.

Planted using the Scotscape fabric semi-hydroponic system, this one has thrived, offering exuberant colour and textures.

SUCCULENTS

This wall of plants showcases varieties that thrive in a dry environment. It includes succulents such as sedum and sempervivum, but also grasses and herbs such as *Festica* gluca, thyme and rosemary.

TOWER OF PLANTS

This tower of plants is a show feature at the Scotscape nursery. Resembling a large piece of living sculpture, it's an independent structure, four metres tall. It was built by driving large posts into the ground and building a freestanding timber frame to bear the weight of the plants. Similar approaches could be used if an existing wall is not structurally strong enough to bear the weight of a living wall, or to incorporate as a feature to hide something else from view.

Built using the Scotscape fabric semi-hydroponic system, the tower includes plants to emphasise height, such as tall grasses, *Stipa* 'horse tails' at the top.

BASEMENT WALL

If you're trapped in the basement doing laundry, what better way to lift your spirits than to gaze out onto a green wall? This simple fern wall was designed by Kate Gould and contains no less than seven different plant species. It was installed using the ANS Global soil-based system.

LIGHT WELL COURTYARD SPACE

This urban light well offered a blank and boring wall space just a few metres from the rear lower ground floor window and main ground floor balcony of the home. The owner, an interior designer, and her husband both originally from Scotland, decided they'd prefer to re-create a Scottish glen scene complete with an insect box and birdhouses.

Planted using the Biotecture hydroponic system, the 18 square metre wall
has been growing successfully for four years. It is maintained monthly by Scotscape for pruning, to be checked for pests and disease and to monitor the feeding and watering system. The owner prunes occasionally, removes any dead leaves and keeps a sharp eye on the ivy, which has a tendency to take over.

Also featured is a dark-leaved heuchera, which offers contrast, an interesting leaf shape and a pop of purple colour. Sadly, it is prone to Vine Weevil – a black beetle pest – so the plant will be removed.

The wall is reminiscent of the forests and woodlands in Scotland, even down to the dark, damp corners! The owner decided not to choose great flowering varieties of plants, but to keep the wall to many interesting different shades of green, with a few purple-leaved plants included for contrast and depth. With an almost architectural-like feel to the wall, the main consideration was given to interesting leaf shapes, patterning within the plants themselves and variation in textures. The owner wanted the wall to look as natural as possible, with no obvious lines of design or patterning in the plant arrangement. The wall doesn't get much sun at all, especially in the lower sections, so it required plants that are happy to grow in these conditions.

This living wall shows clearly that even the smallest space can offer a green perspective. As an Interior Designer, the owner is always thinking about vistas or views through from one room to another. Here she has treated the outside terrace with the living wall as another room and extension of the house and the wall itself is like a piece of living art. The wall, with LED uplighters set flush into the grey sandstone paving slabs, is a dramatic conversation piece at night.

Chapter 4

FOR EATING

Gardening vertically presents an excellent opportunity to grow fruit, herbs and vegetables in a restricted space. Not only will an edible wall, packed with lettuces, leaves, herbs, strawberries and dwarf tomatoes make a great talking point, but it deals neatly with the problem of rabbits. Rabbits can't climb.

Now, even the most space-restricted urban gardener can eat seasonally and hyper-locally. You can grow-your-own using these vertical gardening techniques and ideas.

EDIBLE HIGH RISE

While this 9-metre tall living wall herb tower offered more herbs than a family could possibly eat in a year, it showed the potential for edible gardening on a restricted, vertical plane.

Designed by Patrick Collins and Laurie Chetwood for the DIY store B&Q and installed by Willerby Landscapes as a show garden, the concept was to explore the potential for vertical allotment gardening and to inspire people to grow their own vegetables even with limited space.

Abundant plant boxes at each balcony level included tomatoes, peppers, brassicas and edible flowers, while the walls, planted using the Biotecture hydroponic system, boasted a tapestry of herbs. The whole tower was entirely self-sufficient and included rainwater harvesting, a thermal chimney, solar panels and a wind turbine.

FRESHLY PREPPED GARDEN

A contemporary take on the kitchen garden brings a whole new meaning to locavore eating and grown-close-to-home. Every plant in the garden is edible! Designed by Patricia Fox for her company Aralia Design, this is a courtyard garden with an outdoor kitchen.

Featuring a hardwood deck floor, granite countertops and fully functioning kitchen including a wine fridge, the courtyard included raised growing beds clad in tropical Massaranduba hardwood, planted with herbs for making smoothies, teas and salads and a small selection of fruits, including Calamondin oranges, lemons, apples and pears in the main growing boxes. Overhead, strawberries and tomatoes grew in hanging colanders, while a very wide selection of salad leaves as well as a few runner beans grew from the vertical walls. The walls were planted using the Biotecture hydroponic growing system with an automatic irrigation and feeding system, which is ideal for compact spaces.

CITRUS COURTYARD

This show garden was designed to celebrate the county of Kent as the 'Garden of England', a place where fruit crops flourish. It showcases the production of a diverse range of fruit crops against a background of climate change, water sustainability and locavore eating.

A modern courtyard garden features an outdoor dining area and ribbons of vertically-grown strawberries as a focal point in the living wall. Designed by Mandy Buckland for Hadlow College, a renowned land-based centre of learning, the vertical elements were planted using the ANS Global soil-based system. Easily adaptable for an urban garden, this design would work well in a small city garden for owners interested in seasonal fruit and herb production.

EAT LANDSCAPE, GROWING TOGETHER

Designed by Emily Ross of Eat Landscape, this garden offers a contemporary take on gardening in small spaces – including a 1.85 square metre vertical wall – and using that small space to produce vegetables.

Raised beds made from simple reclaimed scaffolding boards feature ruby chard, purple sage and red perilla, which were picked up by the vertical garden growing up the wall and by resin bound gravel stripes that ran through the garden. Planted using the ANS Global soil-based system, the wall includes cabbage, chard, red perilla, turnip, alpine strawberries and herbs.

POTENTIAL FEAST GARDEN

While raised beds and climbing plants offer options for cultivating vegetables in a small space, another choice is to use the walls. Recessed vertical vegetable beds maximise the use of space and present attractive, living pictures.

In this contemporary outdoor dining space designed by Raine Clarke-Willis and Fiona Godman-Dorington, the edible living pictures, featuring herbs and salad leaves were planted using the compost-based Vertigarden system. For easy home use, installation of an irrigation system is recommended to ensure optimum water and feeding.

"We all usually focus on the produce but actually, the texture, the flowers and the form of many of these edible plants are really beautiful and they look very natural planted alongside perennials and shrubs. So we're trying to say, you don't need an allotment to have produce, if you've got a small garden, just put everything together," said Clarke-Willis.

WALL POCKETS

If it's all about food in your house, these simple wall pockets from Burgon and Ball offer an easy, quick and practical method to get your edible green wall growing fast.

Made from durable fabric with and waterproof back panel and holes in the bottom of the upper level pockets to allow water to drip through to lower layers of plants, the Verti-plant pockets are easy to install and use. Just screw them to a wall or fence, fill the pockets with compost, plant your edibles, water and watch them grow.

Here, the pockets are bursting with chives, oregano, sage, parsley and mint.

HERB SQUARES, ROOFTOP WORKPLACE GARDEN

If your space is restricted but your appetite for greenery and edible walls is not, this herb wall is a fabulous idea for any sunny space. Designed by Patricia Fox, the wall offers a series of herb squares, envisioned as an herbal tea bar, where you can pick fresh herbs and immediately make tea nearby. The wall was planted using the ANS Global soil-based system and includes many forms of mints, including lemon, chocolate, ginger and pineapple.

Chapter 5

LIVING PICTURES AND SMALLER PROJECTS

Bigger is not necessarily always better. While an expansive green wall will always attract attention, beauty can also be found in detail. For those blessed with only very restricted outdoor space or those with an eye for the miniature, vertical gardens offer plenty of options.

They're easier to install and easier to maintain than their larger cousins and can often be portable. Think of miniature living walls like living pictures, a canvas that changes as it grows, or one that you can redesign without too much effort.

YELLOW COURTYARD

In this cheerful yellow summer garden, designer Mike Harvey set out to create high impact with low cost. The garden is just 50 square metres, the size of a small city garden, designed for a professional couple looking to create a low maintenance, outdoor room.

The Yorkstone path was built from less expensive, irregular shaped pieces, while the rocking chairs were made from up-cycled pallets. The yellow wall adds a cheerful hue for those otherwise less-than-sunny summer days, while the small living picture, breaks up the expanse of colour and links it to the garden.

All the plants Harvey chose were drought tolerant, including the succulents - sedums, sempervivums and euphorbia - used to great effect in the miniature living wall picture.

SUCCULENT PANELS

Peter Reader designed and built these miniature succulent mosaic panels as a flower show demonstration. Planted with sedum, *Sempervivum* 'Sir William,' arachnoideum, *Arachnoideum rubin* and *Tectorum rubin*, the panels were a hit with viewers and continue to thrive in his garden at home, requiring minimal maintenance.

Succulents are a great choice for living pictures as they grow slowly, offer a multitude of colours and textures and do not require much watering. If plants get too leggy, then trim or remove the plant and add a new one.

STEP-BY-STEP

For a satisfying project, make your own miniature living picture. Start with a shadow box and frame – buy one or make your own – and then coat with varnish or waterproof wood preservative. Depth of the shadow box should be about 40 mm. Drill plenty of drainage holes in the bottom and cover with permeable horticultural membrane. Staple it into place.

Sub-divide the shadow box using lightweight battens into smaller boxes. Fill the frame with good, lightweight potting soil. Cover the soil with another layer of permeable horticultural membrane. Staple this to the frame edge and the sub-dividing battens. This will hold the soil and the plants in place.

Now make your frame. Treat with varnish or wood preservative. Frames can either be flush with the shadow box, or have an overhang. Affix the frame to the box.

Make small holes in the membrane and plant your sempervivums. They will expand and grow together, locking one another into place. Water the plants and leave flat, in the sun, for at least four weeks, preferably more. Then, slowly, over the course of another four to six weeks, raise the frame to the horizontal position. Hang on a solid surface that can bear the weight.

CONTOURED STRIPES

The very organic feel to this 35 square metre garden, designed by Paul Hensey, is created by concrete walls 2.2-metres high that resemble billowing, open curtains, juxtaposed with slivers of living wall that appear to be a continuation of the flowerbeds growing vertically. Loose planting and a strong sense of movement in the garden merge the horizontal and the vertical.

GREEN STRIPES

Even the smallest piece of vertical greenery adds a contemporary vibe to this garden by designer Mark Gregory. Gregory chose to juxtapose the hard, grey finish of concrete walls, with soft narrow stripes of green, playing both with colour and texture. Using the Biotecture hydroponic system, *Pratia pedunculata* grew happily on the wall, while planters at the foot of the wall and nearby beds contained abundant edibles, including salad leaves, Pak choi, beans, tomatoes, fennel, chives and sage.

These narrow wall strips would work perfectly in a garden with restricted space, particularly for growing herbs.

RED, WHITE AND BLUE

Using one of the many modular systems available, this cheerful, summery design in red, white and a touch of blue is easy to change by replacing highlight plants. It includes pelargoniums, nicotiana, impatiens, lobelia and ivy.

BOUGAINVILLEA PANEL

Here is another good example of breaking up hard design elements with a living wall panel. This vibrant pink *bougainvillea* 'Barbara Karst' panel, mixed with the grass *Carex flacca* was designed by Esra Parr and planted using the Easiwall system from Treebox. The living wall panel introduces a touch of wild into a structured garden and breaks up the strong, vibrant blue of the walls.

MOSS PANELS

These striking contemporary moss panels are easy to make at home. For this project, the designers DeakinLock had a Perspex manufacturer form up the bright pink edging, but you could make the frame from any material yourself. Then affix to a backing of marine-grade plywood at the back. Fill the frame to 2/3 depth with soaked Oasis flower arranging foam. Order cushion moss from your local florist and pin it to the Oasis. Mist regularly with water when dry and display in a shady or semi-shaded part of your garden.

MODULAR PLASTIC

This green wall ecosystem was used by designer Tomaz Bavdez in a futuristic garden, designed to show the inter-connected nature of life, from processing and recycling waste, to using human sweat equity from the power of a person turning the pedals of an exercise bicycle, to pump waste water to water the living walls.

Living walls were planted using a Slovenian system from Humko Bled, which features *Acorus gramineus* 'Ogon' grasses in a custom Humko substrate planting medium made of made of diatomite clay, perlite, pomice, zeolite and coco peat. The living walls were fed by drip irrigation pipes with water and fertiliser.

LIME GREEN STRIPE

Even a small living wall space can allow you to play with colour. In this panel, grown using the ANS Global soil-based system, designed by Kate Gould, a vivid lime green stripe of *Heuchera* 'Lime Marmalade' is juxtaposed with *Euphorbia robbiae*, *Fragaria vesca* and *Pachysandra terminalis*.

PANEL WITH PAVING SLABS

In this show garden designed by Caroline E. Butler, a creeping perennial *Soleirolia soleirolii* (syn *Helxine soleirolii*) was used to create the vertical green panels. The plant offered a soft contrast to the recycled paving stones made by Bradstone, used in an unconventional way to build a wall.

BURGON AND BALL VERTI-PLANT® PANELS

These rainbow-hued Verti-plant® small panel systems are made by Burgon and Ball and allow you to grow a miniature garden on any vertical surface strong enough to bear the weight of the panels. Made from lightweight durable fabric, they include holes in the top two layers to allow water to drip through to plants below.

While the Verti-plant® pouch is waterproof, overwatering may cause surface damage as excess water drips from the bottom. Be careful and water moderately!

Simply fill the pockets with compost, plant your herbs, veggies, fruits or flowers and create an instant miniature, hanging garden.

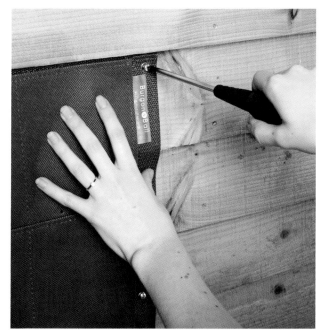

DESIGN LIVING ARCH, PATIO SETTING

This recessed timber archway was set into the fence in the garden of a city house with a small courtyard garden. It was installed using the hydroponic ANS Global system, with a waterproof, breathable membrane installed underneath to prevent rotting. It's a good example of using the vertical plane to add simple interest without eating up valuable space.

SUCCULENT FRAME STEP-BY-STEP

Ultimately satisfying, make your own miniature, hanging garden with this mosaic of succulents *Sempervivums* 'Ruby Heart', calcareum, arachnoideum and kakariki.

Follow these simple steps:
1. Make oak frame.
2. Attach chicken wire with nail gun.
3. Trim excess wire.
4. Put layer of sphagnum moss, then a layer of all-purpose compost, firmed down.
5. Then another layer thinly of sphagnum moss.
6. Cut a plastic membrane to fit and then place chicken wire over and attach (this is now the back of the frame). Turn over to plant.
7. To get an idea of the design, place containers in pattern you'd like.
8. Remove plants from pots and break up carefully to small pieces with roots.
9. Make holes with a dibber or similar gardening tool and then plant carefully.
10. We chose diagonal stripes infilled with contrasting colour.
11. Gradually plant in the design.
12. When finished mist with water.
13. Allow frame to stay flat for two weeks for plants to root and settle in.
14. Then place on wall and mist when needed.

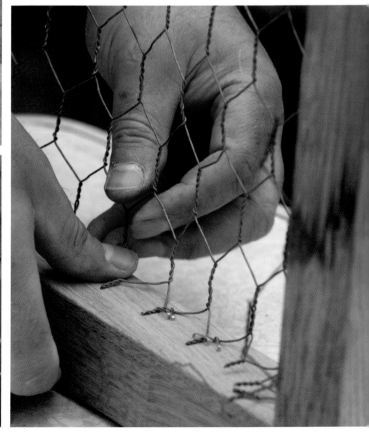

Chapter 6

IN CONTAINER SYSTEMS

Another approach to creating striking green walls, one that provides immediate coverage and colour, is to use one of the several container systems available worldwide.

Generally, these consist of frames which feature designated spaces to hold plant pots. Installation generally requires affixing the framework to the wall and a drainage channel at the foot of the wall if the watering system is a drip one. These container systems mean that you can build a living wall quickly and easily, by simply slotting mature pots into slots. It also means that you can change your display seasonally, for colour or when plants die, and you can grow a diverse range of plants each in their own preferred soil or planting medium, ensuring a vibrant, healthy wall.

ATLANTIS GRO-WALL™

This balcony exterior green wall was planted using the modular Atlantis Gro-Wall™ System. It allows users to add units to easily expand the display, while plants can be grown vertically or angled at 90, 62.5 and 45 degrees. Made from recycled materials, the Gro-Wall™ features built-in irrigation Individual Plant Irrigation system, which virtually eliminates any run-off, but allows plants to be fed and watered by a drip system from the plant above.

Plants grown on this floor-to-ceiling balcony green wall include a wide range of succulents.

LANDTECH SOILS

Featuring 168 plants, including hosta, toad lilies and ivy, this expansive green wall covers the end of a small courtyard garden. Created using the Landtech Soils Bin Fen Green Wall Modular system, it features built-in irrigation and fertilisation. Each pot has a nozzle, which drips for two minutes morning and evening.

Plants are grown in pots, which are about four-inches in diameter, in the planting medium supplied by Landtech, a free-draining sandy soil. They are simple to hook into and out of the support structure, which makes it easy to change the planting plan for seasonal colour and variation.

PIXEL-GARDEN

The Pixel-Garden green wall system is a simple modular affair that allows users to choose the size of their planting area by simply adding more pots.

It does not require any special installation, other than a simple wooden frame, sturdy enough to hold the Pixel-Garden pots, attached to the wall or fence.

Once the frame is in place, screw in the Pixel-Garden pot holders, clicking each one together with its neighbour. Thread the irrigation pipe through the top line of pots and add drip taps. Then, just drop in your pots for an immediate living wall panel.

Chapter 7

BEHIND THE SCENES: HOW TO DO IT

As confusing and complex as vertical gardening systems may seem, in reality the multitude of options available divide into three types: soil-based plastic pockets or modules, soil-based fabric or felt membranes, and the hydroponic systems, which have no soil at all and rely upon water and fertiliser delivered directly to the plants from a tank system to keep them healthy.

Each present with its own challenges and benefits, but some of the most important issues to consider are questions of weight and water, structural decay and the position of your green wall.

The boundary where you intend to grow a living wall must be strong enough to bear the weight of the infrastructure needed. Add the weight of wet, mature plants and this means a flimsy fence that waves in the wind will not stand up to the added strain presented when a living wall is installed.

Your first task is to secure your fence or wall. Your second is to assess how the living wall might affect the structural integrity of the fence or wall, or if the system you choose will keep an air pocket between the green wall and your existing structure. Do you need to install a waterproof membrane first?

Hydroponic systems are usually more expensive to install, but they offer the benefit of automated precision feeding and watering to maximise longevity and health of your wall. Soil-based systems, which can also be precision fed by drip lines, tend to offer a wider choice of plants that will thrive. When considering soil-based systems, it is important to consider soil and root health, as well as the way that plants' roots interact with one another, forming microbial colonies.

VIRIDIWALL™ PANELS BY VERTOLOGY

Viridiwall™ is a hydroponic living wall system. This means that plants receive all their nutrients – both water and food – via an irrigation system. The panels are simply there to anchor the plants.

Viridiwall™, which is available in panels of many different sizes, is made from two kinds of horticultural mineral fibres that drain well and allow air and water to circulate efficiently, both important to encourage optimal plant growth. A black 100 per cent recyclable rigid polypropylene plastic casing covers this fibre.

Line pressure drippers run throughout the Viridiwall™ panels, delivering precisely the amount of water and food needed. Typically, the Viridiwall™ uses around 1 litre of water per square metre of plants per day in a temperate climate and this, as well as nutrients, is supplied by the Basebox™ Irrigation Equipment that is supplied with the wall. This can be monitored remotely.

Viridiwall™ must either be built into a wall, or attached to its own freestanding steel framework. This framework creates an air gap between any existing wall and the living wall. A drainage membrane and backing boards are also installed, before Viridiwall™ panels are hung in place.

Plants are grown on vertical racking in the Vertology nursery for a minimum of eight weeks before installation.

PLANT BRICKS BY VERTOLOGY

Plantbricks™ offer a flexible method to get into tight corners. Made from lightweight horticultural mineral fibres, they offer more flexible coverage for projects where simple flat panels simply won't work – curved walls, steeply-sloped roofs or walls, and other design elements such as stonework or wooden accents where precision planting is required.

Each brick measures just 24 cm long by 10 cm wide and 5 cm deep. Nutrients and water are delivered to the plants by pressured irrigation lines, running from the same system as the Viridiwall™ panels.

VIRIDITROUGH™ BY VERTOLOGY

These troughs from Vertology are designed for trailing plants. They offer an easy way to install a hydroponic green wall in a less intensive way. Plants are rooted in a special hydroponic loose planting medium, which resembles small stones but is made from expanded recycled glass. As the plants grow and trail downwards, they camouflage the troughs below, providing extensive green coverage. While an irrigation and feeding tank remains necessary, the troughs also incorporate a hidden water reservoir at the bottom for optimum access to water between irrigation times.

BIOTECTURE BIOWALL HYDROPONIC SYSTEM

The Biowall system from Biotecture offers a panel-based hydroponic solution for large and small-scale green walls. Plants are rooted in GRODAN, a stone wool made from natural, volcanic basalt rock. The density of GRODAN means that water, air and nutrients can circulate recirculate through the growing medium, offering a stable, healthy growing environment for plants.

Plants are rooted and then grown on in Biowall panels in a greenhouse for eight weeks before being installed, along with an automated watering and fertilising system. Used both commercially and in residential settings, indoors and out, Biowall has very low water needs – typically 1 litre per m2 per day – in temperate climates, which only adds to its green credentials.

SCOTSCAPE HYBRID SEMI-HYDROPONIC AND SOIL SYSTEM

The Scotscape Living Wall is a textile lightweight semi-hydroponic modular panel system, made from a patented advanced geotextile fabric with a waterproof back panel. Each square metre holds 49 plants in individual pockets. Plants are watered and fed by a dripline, through the fabric.

Panels can be fitted to flat or curved surfaces and are planted on site in the compost-peat mix in which they are grown at the nursery. Once planted, their roots grow together and into the fabric and no more soil is added, unless the wall is exposed to extremes of the elements, such as heavy rainfall or high winds, which may cause the soil to deteriorate. From planting onwards, Scotscape green wall plants receive their nutrition from a Dosatron, which is a machine that mixes plant food with water.

Plants are easy to replace. Simply tug one out and pop another one in the hole. Some clients choose to change a certain number of their plants regularly for colour or to add flowers, but the majority of plants remain in place for the longer term.

ANS GLOBAL SOIL SYSTEM

The plastic tray module soil-based system from ANS Global is easy to adapt to any scale, from huge commercial projects worldwide, to small, moveable interior green wall panels in office and residential spaces.

The infrastructure behind ANS Global living walls is relatively simple. First, wooden batons are affixed to the existing structure. To prevent moisture damage, an impermeable membrane is added next. Then, hanging brackets, fixing rails and a drain for any excess moisture run-off are installed, before the pre-planted modules are hung in place.

Plants grow in a natural soil mix, a bespoke recipe containing coir, wood fibre, green waste and natural compost, and are planted 12 to a tray. Each has a piece of capillary matting to facilitate water movement from the back of the module to the roots of the plant. Trays take from 4 to 12 weeks to grow on in the ANS Global nurseries, where they hang in a nearly vertical position. Each tray features a hidden cavity for a drip water pipe, which then delivers water on an automated schedule. Fertiliser and pest control can also be delivered through the system during maintenance visits. About 10 per cent of plants are replaced annually.

Chapter 8

WHICH PLANTS WHERE?

Gardens are first about people, then the plants they choose. So while your vertical garden should first be an expression of your creativity and taste, it also has to work in the space you have chosen for it. In other words, a vertical garden is no different than a horizontal garden: If you put the wrong plant in the wrong place, it won't grow. So it's no good putting plants that like a wet, shady environment on a wall in full sun. They won't be happy, no matter how much on-demand water and food you give them. Your green wall will be a brown, dead one far sooner than you'd like.

While choosing the right plant for the right place is possibly the most important decision you can make when planning your wall, there are many other important variables to consider, because planting and maintaining a successful living wall is not as easy as doing the same thing on the ground. It requires more precise watering, more precise feeding (sometimes this changes for different parts of the same wall) and regular pruning and checking for disease.

First, living wall plants are under a great deal more stress than those in your conventional flowerbed. They are planted at great density – usually between 30 and 100 plants per square metre, whereas a flowerbed might have between 5 and 9 – which means that you need to keep in mind how they will grow and interact with their neighbours. It's all too easy for the neat, textural tapestry you planted at the outset to quickly get out of hand as larger plants swamp their neighbours, causing die back and ugly empty brown patches.

Because we look at living walls at eye level, our tolerance for bare patches is low. In order for your wall to look good, it must appear as a lush, vibrant tapestry of plants, knit closely together. This means that unless you choose the right plants for the right place, ones that are disease resistant and can adapt to growing on the vertical plane with restricted root space, you'll constantly be replacing dead ones.

Disease is another factor to consider. When plants are crowded, disease can spread rapidly. Some plants are more susceptible to aphids, Vine Weevil or millipedes munching at their roots. It's best to avoid these, no matter how pretty the plants might look at the outset.

Then there are plants that suffer from constant die back even as they produce new growth – some grass species look constantly messy because they are thick with straw, while hosta lose their leaves in winter, leaving holes that won't be filled until spring, so they're best not planted in great swathes.

For a wall that will look good all year long, it's best to choose 95 per cent evergreen plants with plenty of different textures so that you're not left with empty spots during the winter months. For seasonal colour you can add perennials, but do so in a matrix planting scheme, among evergreens that will cover them when they die down.

Next look for low-growing varieties, ideally less than 50 cm tall at maturity. Choose plants that are disease resistant and long-lived: You don't want to be replacing large numbers of plants every year, since you'll be replacing plants every three to five years as it is. While regular maintenance is a necessity, and many companies offer maintenance contracts, you still want to keep it to a minimum.

First choose your plants by site condition – full sun, full shade, windy, sea spray, or even a combination depending on location within your planting area – then turn your attention to finding a balance of colour and textural contrast, flowering highlights and seasonal changes. You can also opt to plant by theme, such as a tropical wall, herbs, edibles, pizza garden, salad garden, tea garden, cocktail party planting or for spring and autumn colour.

Here are some plant suggestions for your garden in the sky.

HERBS:
Basil, Bay, Caraway, Chamomile, Chives, Coriander, Curry plant, Dill, Lavender, Lemon balm, Lemongrass, Marjoram, Mint, Oregano, Parsley, Rosemary, Sage, Sorrel Tarragon, Thyme.

EDIBLE PLANTS:
Chard, Cherry tomatoes, Dwarf cabbages, English spinach, Lettuces, Radishes, Rocket, Silverbeet, Small Chillies, Strawberries, Watercress.

PLANTS FOR SUN:

Achillea, Acorus, *Armeria maritima*, Bergenia, Bidens, *Calamintha nepeta*, Carex, *Convolvulus cneorum*, *Coreopsis verticillata*, Crassula, Dianthus, Echeveria, Erica, Erigeron, Erysimum, *Eschscholzia californica* Californian poppy, Euphorbia, *Festuca glauca*, Geranium, *Hebe pinguifolia*, Helianthemum, Lavender, Liriope, Lobelia, Pansy, Pelargonium, Petunia, Rosemary, Salvia, *Sanguisorba officinalis*, Santolina, Sedum, Solidago, *Stachys byzantina*, *Stipa calamagrostis*, Sempervivums, Thyme, Veronica, Westringia.

PLANTS FOR SHADE:

Adiantum, *Ajuga reptans*, *Asplenium*, Begonia, Bergenia, *Carex elata*, *Chlorophytum comosum*, *Cyrtomium falcatum*, Epimedium, Erica, Euphorbia, Fuchsia, *Hedera helix* ivy, *Helleborus*, Heuchera, Heucherella, Hosta, Impatiens, *Lamium maculatum*, *Liriope muscari*, *Pachysandra terminalis*, *Pellaea falcata*, *Phlebodium aureum* 'Blue Star', Polystichum, *Polypodium vulgare*, *Pteris cretica*, *Pteris tricolor*, Sarcococca, Skimmia, Snowdrop, *Soleirolia soleirolii*, Tiarella, *Vinca minor*, Viola (some Viola plants will cope with sun or shade).

PLANTS FOR TROPICAL AREAS:

Achimenes erecta, Acorus, Aeschynanthus (*lipstick plant*), *Aglaonema*, *Anthurium scherzerianum*, *Aucuba japonica*, Begonia, Bromeliads, Chlorophytum, *Cleyera japonica*, *Codiaeum croton*, Cordyline, Dieffenbachia, Dracaena, *Episcia cupreata*, *Fatsia japonica*, Ferns, Fittonia, *Hypoestes*, Limonium, *Maranta leuconeura*, Mondo grass, Orchids, Peperomia, Philodendron, *Phlebodium aureum*, *Pteris cretica*, *Saxifraga stonifera*, *Solenostemon*, Spathiphyllum, *Syngonium podophyllum*, Tradescantia.

Chapter 9

VERTICAL GARDENING FOR THE LONG HAUL

While green roofs have been a part of the horticultural vernacular since the 1960s when they first started to appear in Germany, Austria and Switzerland on a large scale, living walls have only really gained traction over the last 10 years. Will they last?

Living walls were slow to get going. While the idea was good, poor planting systems, inappropriate plant choices and lack of proper care and maintenance contributed to many spectacular failures in the nascent industry, pioneered in France by Patrick Blanc and his felt-based system. But as scientists, designers and horticulturalists have refined their approaches, larger and larger swathes of our urban vertical planes are turning green and staying green.

With positive results from research into the benefits of green walls, both at an environmental and health level, and anecdotal evidence from people exposed to living walls in their workplace and city environment, they are becoming an integral part of any urban planning and design process. They are also crossing the boundary from commercial and infrastructure uses to residential applications. Developers, in particular, have realised the appealing nature of living walls and the value they add to a property. In this way, new homeowners are inheriting green walls when they buy a house.

Scotscape recently completed a very large living wall project in central London. A developer had bought a row of five mews houses. The company proceeded to retain the external walls but completely renovate inside. But along the back of the mews houses there was a nine metre tall wall too close to the rear windows, leaving no space for outdoor living, nor gardens. Solid, but extremely ugly, this wall was no selling feature. The developer decided to improve the otherwise ugly wall with vertical strips of living wall, interspersed with cedar panels. The houses sold quickly.

A useful way to look at the future of living walls is in the short, medium and long-terms.

Short-term sustainability has a great deal to do with maintenance. Green walls are only successful when correctly planted – right plant, right place – and regularly maintained. Vertical planting places plants under a great deal more stress than in a conventional garden bed. This means that in order to thrive, plants need more attention than they would otherwise. Correct irrigation and nutrients delivered at the right time, to the right plant, as well as frequent pruning and checking for disease are the basic levels of care needed to maintain a successful green wall. Soil, root health and the microbe community among roots are also important to consider, which means that your wall needs to be accessible.

Once the jungle effect is allowed to take over, not enough light reaches the smaller plants at the back of the wall and a die off effect begins to occur, eventually leaving large brown patches.

Dead plants and gaps quickly turn a living wall from a marvel to a mess. Frequent pruning, weeding and replacement of any dead plants is imperative if your wall is to thrive from the short-term to the long-term.

In the medium-term, living walls will be sustainable if they become a fundamental part of urban planning and design – "green urbanism". While they are still a relatively new phenomenon, worthy of comment and sometimes awe, city planners need to incorporate greenery into every piece of new design – be that high rise apartments, shopping malls, office buildings, bridges or even highway overpasses. Only once they become such an integral part of city living, will their future become assured. In other words, when urban populations decide that they can't live without vertical greening elements and even urban food production, then their medium-to long-term livelihood will be assured.

But it takes more than great ideas and academic research papers that tell us how important greening our cities is to our future, to affect permanent change. It will take the collaboration of urban planners, engineers, ecologists, psychologists, landscape architects, sociologists, transport planners, architects and garden designers to create green master plans to design the successful, sustainable green cities of the future.

Transport for London has taken the idea to heart and is putting it into action. In an effort to improve air quality where particulate matter pollution is highest, TfL's Future Streets Incubator Fund as well as the London Clean Air Fund have been involved with four major permanent green wall initiatives, as well as providing funding for temporary green screens to camouflage construction sites. They have installed 50 plant towers on a particularly busy road that connects east to west, and have started to plant some 500 new trees slated for the capital.

For long-term sustainability, it comes to a simple cost versus benefit conversation.
If the perceived environmental benefits of green walls, using any of the many systems available today, is deemed to be worth the added initial expense, then living walls and vertical greening initiatives will be sustainable. Product will influence policy. So, if cost savings from heating, cooling and less degradation of buildings are also thrown into the equation, then green walls become increasingly attractive, especially in warmer climates where they offer substantial savings for air conditioning. Add any potential tax incentives to the equation and suddenly green walls become sustainable by many measures.

The life span of the various planting systems is an important consideration when endeavouring to assess the long-term prospects of green walls. No comparative study exists to tell us which one will last the longest. However, it's safe to assume that the more complicated the system, the less economically sustainable it is. Continued innovation in the design of living wall systems, including added thermal insulating and fire retardant properties will determine the long-term sustainability of projects to vertically green our cities.

Chapter 10

CLIMBERS, CREEPERS AND ESPALIERED

Long before technology caught up with gardening, we have been gardening vertically for millennia using more traditional methods. Easiest and chief among these is to grow climbing plants up an existing surface.

There are two kinds of plants suitable for directly greening a surface: those that adhere to the wall using suckers or adhesive pads and those that climb a trellis, wall or other lightweight form of support. Trellises are generally made from wood, in smaller and domestic settings, but this does have a tendency to decay. Other options include wire mesh and simple string or wire, threaded from screw to screw. In larger or commercial settings, climbing support structures are often made from stainless steel rope, rods or wire mesh.

Whichever way these plants choose to climb, they like their roots planted in soil, in a bed at the foot of the wall. This means that it's an easy project. Choose your climber, suited to your aspect, prepare the soil and planting hole to make the most welcoming environment possible and pop it in. Within a few short years, you should have a robust green wall.

There are a wide variety of climbers to choose from, suitable for any number of climates. Think ivy, climbing hydrangea, Virginia creeper, abundant roses, wisteria, hops, honeysuckle and clematis, just for a start. The list of climbing plants is as endless as your particular position. Is your spot sunny, shady, dry, sandy, loamy, damp, windy or salty?

There are, for example, 16 species of ivy with over 400 varieties, some of which can reach over 30-metres in height. But most climbing plants will not reach this height which means they are less suited for commercial settings such as apartment towers and other high rise buildings, and more suited for the domestic context.

Even without the substantial infrastructure required for living walls, climbers will offer heating and cooling benefits to the structures where they are grown, as well as protection from decay caused by expansion and contraction. Typically, it is best to plant deciduous climbers such as wisteria on south facing walls so that in summer the leaves offer cooling benefits and in winter the sun can strike the wall to offer heat. On north facing walls, an evergreen such as Boston or English ivy offers the most benefits.

However, ivy (English ivy in particular) must be handled with care, taking into account your climate and the condition of your masonry as it can quickly become invasive and cause damage to bricks that are not in good condition. Ivy is especially problematic near gutters, rooflines, windows and paintwork where it can cause damage. While it will offer a fast growing and classic green façade, with an endearing English country house appeal, you must prune ivy regularly and keep it under tight control.

PLUMBAGO

Plumbago 'auriculata' is an evergreen shrub with striking blue flowers. Native to South Africa, it thrives in temperate and tropical climates, or indoors in a greenhouse. Plumbago, also known as Leadwort, can grow to 10 feet tall and naturally creates a waterfall shape if not trained against a fence or arbour . It needs full sun to produce its abundant flowers, which attract butterflies, but if it's really happy in its environment, it can become invasive. It produces a sticky substance from its flowers, which makes pruning a messy job and all parts of the plant are poisonous.

PYRACANTHA

Commonly known as Firethorn, Pyracantha is a thorny, evergreen shrub that has a pretty white flower in spring and abundant yellow, orange or red berries in autumn and winter. It attracts bees to its spring flowers and birds, which like to eat the berries in winter. Pyracantha only flowers and therefore produces berries on old wood, which means it should be pruned with care to not remove too much of the previous year's growth. It will grow in most soil types, but does not like to be flooded. It prefers full sun to partial shade. It is surprisingly versatile for a shrub with a woody trunk, as it can be trained to grow up walls, fences, arbours or even espaliered, in the way of a fruit tree. It can also be pruned to create a thick, full hedge.

TRACHELOSPERMUM

Sometimes known as Star Jasmine, Trachelospermum has wonderful white, star-shaped scented flowers and is a woody, evergreen climber that is frost hardy. It thrives in full sun to dappled shade and is a vigorous climber, sometimes reaching more than 25 feet. It is a self-clinging, twining climber that will make its own way once established. However, it can be trained along a fence to give the effect of an espaliered tree, (picture 14), or tied onto a fence to create a flowering green screen (picture 15).

Trachelospermum can be trained and pruned to grow around pillars (picture 16) to create wonderful, soft, fragrant columns.

CLEMATIS

Whole books have been written about clematis. There are close to 300 species of this woody-stemmed plant, one of the most popular of all garden plants. Originally found in the wild in China, clematis thrive in sun, part sun and shade, depending on the variety you choose, but they do like to keep their roots in a moist, cool place. So, if you're planning to plant a clematis in full sun to grow up a baking wall, be sure to keep it watered. Also, take great care when planting, as young plants are very fragile.

Pic 20 – Clematis can easily be trained to grow up pergola columns, intertwining with other climbing plants such as honeysuckle or hops. They produce a soft, loose, cottage garden style.
Pic 21 – Clematis are equally happy growing along a wall. You may need to provide some form of structure for the clematis to grow up until established – such as strings, wire or a trellis - but beware when tying them up, they are extremely fragile and breakable when young.

There are so many wonderful colours of clematis that it's a nice idea to combine them, so that you benefit from the diversity of flower shapes, flowering times and colours available. Some even have pretty seed pods that offer winter interest, if you leave your pruning until the spring.

There's no hard and fast rule for pruning clematis. Some only flower on old wood, some don't mind being cut right back to their roots. The easiest way to understand what your clematis needs is to wait until mid-spring to prune. If your plant is sending out new green shoots from old vines, leave them. If not, prune them.

ROSES

Is there anything more wonderful than a scented, abundant, tumbling tower of rambling or climbing roses?

The difference between rambling and climbing roses is simply that rambling roses usually flower once a year, in great abundance, while climbing roses flower over the summer, but without such a dramatic display. In order to have flowers over the course of the whole growing season, the ideal is to plant a June-flowering rambler close to a repeat-flowering climbing rose. This way you'll get the initial wow! factor of cascading flowers, followed by the more muted beauty of a trained climbing rose.

To achieve a successful climbing rose with plenty of flowers, you'll need patience. It will take a couple of years for a rose to get established, during which time it might not flower much. It's putting its energy into growing, not flowering. During this time, do not prune the main canes, but train them where you'd like them to go. Generally, roses flower most prolifically if their canes are trained horizontally. Make sure your rose has rich, fertile, well-drained soil and at least six hours of sun daily.

Some roses can grow as tall as 20 feet and these varieties are best used on pergolas and arbors, or trained along walls. All roses require annual and careful pruning. Roses are susceptible to disease and annual pruning will help to keep any disease in check. If you let your climbing or rambling rose grow wildly, you'll be left with a mass of canes and very few flowers.

For that romantic English country house look, think of choosing a rose to frame a window, rather than ivy or other climbing plants to grow up a wall. Or plant a rose at the back of a border bed, with a structure for it to grow up. Train roses against existing garden walls, or encourage them to drape and fall over pergolas.

BOUGAINVILLEA

Originally from South America, bougainvillea is a thorny, ornamental vine that is not frost hardy. Once it becomes established, it likes a slightly acidic, relatively dry environment with plenty of hot sunshine and temperatures that do not dip below 16 degrees Celsius at night, nor over 38 during the day.

Bougainvillea is easily trained and therefore works well for growing along walls where it can maximise exposure to the sun. One of the most common varieties is a vibrant, cheerful tropical pink that will flower for 11 months of the year if planted in the right climate.

IVY

Ivy has a mixed reputation. On the one hand it's attractive, available in many leaf shapes, sizes and colours and easy to grow. On the other, it can easily become invasive, sometimes it causes skin rashes and it can cause damage to paintwork, windows, gutters, drainpipes and crumbling masonry. But if contained, planted prudently and pruned regularly, ivy is a great addition to any vertical gardening scheme.

Ivy offers dense cover, quickly. It will grow up almost any surface. Here a variegated variety offers colour and texture to a pillar.

Around a window, ivy creates a romantic, secret feeling with panes of glass peeping from a dense wall of green. Care should be taken not to allow the ivy to encroach on paint or wooden window frames.

Ivy creates a dense and solid screen when grown over an archway, creating a natural entrance to a different part of the garden.

Ivy can be encouraged to grow up the base of a pedestal of an urn which creates the impression that the urn is floating atop a green pilaster.

CAMELLIA ›

The camellia is an evergreen shrub or small tree, usually grown in a small to medium-sized shrub format. But they can be trained to grow in an ornamental fashion, or espaliered against a wall.

Originally from China and Japan, camellias are also known as the plant that produces tea. But in its ornamental form, it is available from pale pink through to dark red, and more rarely in shades of cream and yellow, with glossy, dark green leaves. Flowers appear in a wide variety of forms from delicate single petal flat bowl or cupped shaped blossoms, to semi-double and double flowered varieties.

While most camellias are happiest in temperate growing regions, recent new camellia varieties can be grown in climate zones where temperatures drop as low as minus 20 degrees Celsius.

The vibrant, glossy dark green leaves create a fabulous graphic design on a wall. However, it is generally not advised to espalier a camellia directly to a wall as they can suffer from heat stress. For the greatest chance of success, train your camellia to a structure parallel to, but about two feet away from the wall to allow air to circulate. With time, it will grow into a remarkable floral sculpture.

Camellias can also be grown as a hedge, creating the most fabulous dense, glossy, tall green screens. Here, shown with a window for framing a garden statue.

NASTURTIUM ›

The nasturtium, long regarded as an edible, bushy annual, is also available as a climber. Happy to grow in poor soil and dry conditions, nasturtiums will scramble over walls and climb a trellis. Nasturtium is sometimes considered to be a noxious weed.

106

‹ IPOMOEA

Otherwise known as Morning Glory, Ipomoea is sometimes considered to be a noxious weed. Available from deep purple to pale pink and white, Morning Glory is a strong climber but has become invasive in some parts of the world.

‹ SWEET PEAS

So reminiscent of the English country garden, sweet peas with their ruffled blossoms are excellent climbers that offer delicate, scented flowers throughout the spring and into early summer. Best grown in rich, well-drained soil in full sun to partial shade up a trellis or strings, sweet peas are excellent for picking and flower arranging. They will perfume a whole room. In order to keep them flowering, you must fertilise them throughout the growing and flowering season and you must pick daily, or every second day to prevent them from going to seed. Sweet peas are susceptible to mildew, so don't plant too close together, leaving space for air to circulate.

‹ WISTERIA

Wisteria is a fabulous plant for adding vertical elements to any garden. Strong, woody, climbing vines can climb up to 20 metres once the plant becomes established. It is happy to wind its way around any available support including pergolas, arbours and up house walls and can be used to create vibrant, scented tunnels. Wisteria prefers fertile, well-drained soil, but will eventually grow almost anywhere. Wisteria flowers in the spring, just before the leaves appear, producing white, yellow or most commonly pale purple pendulous flowers that hang in heavy grape-like bunches. Some species, such as the Chinese Wisteria, produce a fabulous scent.

LABURNUM ›

Producing vivid yellow, pendulous flowers in spring, much like the Wisteria, all parts of the Laburnum are very poisonous. They can be trained to grow up pergolas and their hanging flowers mean that they can be used to create spectacular flowering tunnels, much like the Wisteria.

HOPS

Formerly grown widely as an agricultural crop and used in the crafting of beer as a flavouring and stability agent, hops are now often seen in a horticultural setting. This herbaceous perennial is an aggressive climber, sending up strong, bright green shoots annually that typically grow up strings to heights of 15 metres or more.

ESPALIERED FRUIT

To espalier a tree or shrub is the practice whereby the branches of that tree or shrub are trained into flat, two-dimensional forms. Very often, fruit trees are used for this purpose and they are espaliered against a wall or fence, which can help to increase harvests and ripen fruit, as the wall retains heat overnight. But not all fruit trees are espaliered to a flat surface and they can be freestanding, with their branches trained along wires.

More complicated espalier patterns can take several years to achieve and involve tying the branches to vertical or horizontal wires under tension, during the summer months when the branches are at their most flexible, and removing new growth where necessary to encourage the tree to grow into a desired shape. Trees can be espaliered into many different forms – from those found in formal gardens of the 17th and 18th centuries, to contemporary styles to fit a small urban garden. Espaliers can be trained into V-shapes, T-shapes, vertical lines, curlicues, U-shapes, candelabras and fan shapes, among others.

There are many trees (and shrubs) suitable for the practice of espaliering, but apple and pear trees are seen most commonly because they are long-lived and produce abundant fruit when espaliered.

These are some tree suggestions if you are interested in the espalier technique:
- *Acer palmatum* Japanese Maple
- *Cercis canadensis* Redbud
- *Citrus spp.* Lemon, Orange, Tangerine, etc.
- *Coccoloba uvifera* Sea grape
- *Eriobotrya japonica* Loquat
- *Euonymus alata* Winged Euonymus
- *Ficus carica* Fig
- *Forsythia intermedia* Forsythia
- *Ilex spp.* Hollies, [2] esp. *Ilex cornuta 'Burford'* Burford holly
- *Lagerstroemia indica* Crape myrtle
- *Magnolia grandiflora* Southern magnolia
- *Magnolia stellata* Star Magnolia
- *Malus spp.* Apple, Crabapple, etc.
- *Olea europia* Olive
- *Prunus spp.* Peach, Nectarine, Plum, Almond, etc.
- *Pyrus spp.* Pear
- *Taxus sp.* Yew

While increasing fruit production is often the goal of many espaliered trees, this practice also creates a focal point in any garden, offering exquisite branching patterns in winter and a flat, vertical green screen in summer which can be used as a garden bed divider or to hide unattractive fences, walls or garbage bins.

Chapter 11

HANGING BASKETS AND CONTAINERS

A very simple idea to increase vertical interest in your garden is to include hanging baskets and containers. Baskets introduce a shot of colour, add interest at eye level and are simple to plant and install. Containers, mounted on windowsills, balconies, along walls or on plinths can also add vertical interest and offer a sense of theatre and display.

There are no rules for planting successful hanging baskets and containers. You can choose an explosion of colour and riotous flowers that cascade over the edges for a loose, cottage style, but equally effective is to plant just one colour in abundance. Or even no colour at all – simple clipped box in contemporary planters makes a minimalist, tidy statement.

Don't keep your baskets and planters just for flowers. For anyone with restricted gardening space, they work just as well for herbs, dwarf tomatoes, strawberries and even low-growing vegetables such as chilli peppers, chard and bush beans.

The greatest concern with any container is over or under watering. Because of their restricted root space, plants will dry out more quickly in baskets and containers. On the other hand, if the basket or container does not drain well, they will also suffer if their roots are left to sit in too much water.

To plant a successful hanging basket is simple:
* Choose the right sized basket for your space and the plants you intend to fill it. If the base of the basket will be visible, choose something pretty such as wicker or decorative ironwork. White plastic does not look nice when at eye level.
* Line your basket. There are several ways to do this using sphagnum moss, cocoa liners, burlap liners, a product called Supamoss or even cardboard. You are looking for something that will drain excess water, but will retain moisture.
* Fill your basket half full with potting soil. You might like to add moisture pellets to the planting mix to help with moisture retention.
* Choose one taller central accent for the basket. Next, plant trailing plants to hang over the edge around the sides. Fill in any holes with other, medium height plants of your choice.
* Fill in around the plants with more soil. Add fertiliser sticks. Water. Hang from your wall hook.

Because containers and hanging baskets offer only limited space for plant roots to travel and limited soil in which to plant them, to ensure you get the most from your planting, fertilise with a liquid feed once a fortnight during the summer and water regularly.

There are no rules for hanging baskets. Healthy, abundant plants are what you're after and it doesn't matter if you choose a rainbow of colours or one colour. But if you're planning more than one hanging basket, try to repeat your choice for some continuity and sense of theme. Petunias, geraniums and fuchsia are summer favourites for their strong, vibrant colour and form.

Of course, a hanging basket is a great place to grow a few herbs or other edible plants. They'll be out of the reach of rabbits and squirrels, although they might not look quite as decorative as cascading flowers!

Walls and fences present the perfect neutral backdrop for a shot of interest, introduced through planters and boxes. Along the top of a wall, affixed to a wall or even along windowsills, your canvas for container gardening is endless.

Simple single pots can easily be suspended from any wall, while a group of terracotta pots injects a timeless, rustic feel to any garden and can be a great place to grow herbs or the classic geranium.

For a more contemporary take on container gardening, choose square or rectangle shapes, metallic or brightly coloured finishes and simple repetition of one or two plants.

Don't let a good set of exterior stairs go to waste! Stairs present a great opportunity to display plants or herbs in containers. It's as simple as placing a pot on each level to add vertical interest and lead the eye upwards.

Another good way to add a vertical accent to your garden is to group together several plants in containers on a decorative stand.

If you're going for the wildly eclectic southern California hippie look, then choose a mixed selection of pots. But if you're going for a slightly more curated look, choose one type of pot and vary the size according to height and the plants you choose. An old ladder adds a rustic element when paired with terracotta pots.

Larger containers present the perfect opportunity for a statement plant such as clipped box bushes and trees or an ornamental standard.

Gardening can be whimsical too! This terracotta man presents the perfect place for a tuft of chive hair. While a beautiful outdoor table can also serve as just the place to plant a raised herb garden – easy to plant, easy to pick.

These raised beds provide a good gardening solution for the elderly. Once bending down becomes more pain than gain, it's easy enough to raise garden beds to sitting or standing height.

Chapter 12

STRUCTURES — PERGOLAS, ARBORS, LATTICE AND TRIPODS

The most beautiful gardens and landscapes are those with plenty of contrasting elements. From expansive flowerbeds to hidden corners, cozy nooks with a reading bench to far-reaching views punctuated by majestic trees, or green tunnels that lead your eye to a focal point. Built structural elements can create all of these features in your garden, creating a sense of discovery in an expansive, or even the smallest space.

Pergolas and arbors are exceptionally useful for creating a sense of enclosure and confinement, for separating a little piece of a garden from the remainder. They can act as screens from one garden "room" to another, or shelter for a bench or table. They can act as a structure to encourage climbing plants or create a green tunnel when covered by cascading wisteria, grapes or roses.

Pergolas and arbours can also add a distinct character to your garden. Gently curved, arched, square or tent-shaped, they'll quickly define a space and lift the eye. Choose an Asian-inspired one and you'll introduce a little bit of the east; choose a chunky wooden one cascading with wisteria and you'll bring a little bit of the Mediterranean to your garden; choose a wicker one covered with climbing sweet peas and giant sunflowers and you'll create a quintessential English country cottage garden; choose a dark metal one covered with dense, clipped ivy and your pergola will indicate quiet contemporary.

Lattice-work can be useful in the garden for growing climbing plants and as a semi-transparent screen between one area and another.

Seating arbours offer a moment of respite in any garden. What better way to while away a few minutes or even an afternoon than perched on a bench, surrounded by greenery and flowers?

Metal, wicker, lattice, canvas or wood, arbours offer shelter and serenity, a place to pause and consider the landscape that surrounds them. They can also offer a point of focus in any garden, letting your eye rest and drawing it upwards, away from the horizontal flowerbeds. The sense of enclosure is a pleasant contrast to the open space around.

Pergolas are useful in even the smallest garden. Not only do they lead the eye towards a more distant point, but they can also be used to break up a space into linked but different parts, acting like open gateways.

Wooden pergolas offer the perfect place to grow some of the more woody climbing plants – cascading wisteria, rambling roses and their more restrained climbing rose cousins.

For a looser, more cottage country garden, you can create your own pergola-like tunnel out of willow or hazel whips. Fast-growing and easy to work with, these create good structures for growing lightweight climbing plants such as sweet peas, clematis and hops for that quintessentially country cottage garden feel.

Metal frames offer a more refined take on the chunky wood or loose willow pergola. Because they are precision made, they can introduce symmetry into your garden, when used in repetition.

Metal arches also offer a good structure on which to grow fruit. They are strong enough to support woody plants and the weight of any fruit produced, but lightweight enough to remain decorative without overwhelming the tree. Also, they offer less chance of pests and disease attacking any ripe fruit as unlike wood, they will not rot.

Lattices can be useful in the garden for growing climbing plants and as a semi-transparent screen between one area and another. Surprisingly, for what amounts to a series of pieces of crisscrossed wood, lattices can bring a strong sense of style to your garden.

When made from rustic, knobby grey wood and covered with rambling roses, a lattice adds country charm.

A lattice can offer a growing support for an espaliered fruit tree (a lemon tree for example).

When painted green, a lattice imparts a slightly patchy, camouflage effect, allowing coloured flowers to pop against the green background.

Simple horizontal lines introduce a contemporary feel with clematis or morning glory climbing the structure.

While tripods offer another form of support for growing climbing plants, they also offer a vertical exclamation point of structure in a garden.

Despite their classical shape and slightly Egyptian feel reminiscent of pyramids, tripods can introduce a surprisingly contemporary feel to a garden, especially when painted.

Used in repetition, tripods can create a sense of containment in a garden, like the four corner posts of fencing. Alternatively, when used in a line or avenue, tripods focus the eye on a distant point or the horizon.

When made from lightweight bamboo poles or whips, tripods are useful for growing lighter-weight climbing plants such as sweet peas, all sorts of beans, and even cucumbers and peas.

Chapter 13

SCULPTURAL ELEMENTS, INSTALLATIONS, CRAFT AND ART IN THE GARDEN

Placing sculpture in gardens has a long and noble history.

The grand gardens of renaissance Italy were dotted with pieces of classical sculpture, creating veritable outdoor museums. A little later, from 1643 onwards, Louis XIV, the Sun King, amassed a huge collection in the magnificent gardens at Versailles. Classical gods and goddesses, noble busts, leaping stags, swimming dolphins, simpering angels, nymphs and fauns were all considered suitable subjects for outdoor sculpture.

In the 21st century, subject matter has diversified wildly with monumental abstract works finding homes in contemporary and classical gardens alike. There's a robust industry in modern sculpture pieces of every scale, intended for outdoor display.

Garden sculpture can do many things; it can enhance a landscape when placed in just the right place; it can create a visual axis in a garden space; it can create a focal point in a larger landscape; it can encourage garden visitors to stop their roaming eye, linger and look more closely at the plants and landscape around them; it can draw the eye vertically.

While larger commissioned works are beyond the scale of most gardens and the budgets of all but a few, there are plenty of easy, whimsical and very decorative ways to introduce an installation, craft piece or homemade sculpture into your own garden, adding vertical elements and a focal point just where needed.

The simple cylindrical shape of a pole – bamboo, metal, painted, wood, Perspex, acrylic – can add an easy vertical element to your landscape. Grouped together or planted symmetrically, poles take up little space in the garden, but can be just the ticket to lift the eye or create a focal point.

Left: Minimalist tall bamboo sticks stand as sentinels in a garden, bringing a Japanese flavour to the serene landscape, complete with clean-lined floating steps and a minimalist colour palette in green, white and yellow.

Below: These translucent fluorescent orange acrylic rods of varying heights were planted at the wet edges of a water feature. Inter-planted with Siberian iris, the rods conjured up the colours and feel of an Asian rice paddy.

Right: Simple polished metal poles add a modern twist to traditional planting and introduce a touch of shine into the garden.

Left (below): In this contemporary garden design, cast acrylic rods and tubes create the feeling of a natural cage.

Right (below): A cluster of deep red painted large-gauge bamboo poles offers stark contrast to a backdrop of bright green ferns.

Left (top): Mid-gauge bamboo poles in front of a purple wall impart a contemporary, Asian edge.

Left (bottom): There's no need to hide your birdhouses in a tree – make them a focal point for your garden by creating a birdhouse village in the sky – and inadvertently a piece of contemporary art.

Below: A large piece of bamboo can become the perfect plant stand.

Right (top and bottom): Aztec-inspired paint and embellishments on bamboo poles are reminiscent of Central American windpipes.

Below: A playful oversized take on a child's tin whistle doubles as a windpipe sculpture

Left and below (top): These brightly coloured rain collectors are tubes made from cast acrylic. With their primary colour contemporary vibe, they play off the greens, reds and yellow found in surrounding flowerbeds.

Below (bottom): A simple rising line of graded wooden planks backed by a metal hanging curtain, act as a semi-transparent garden screen.

Above: Sculptural garden elements need not be fine art. These tall, rustic square timber posts are decorated with graffiti style lettering to bring an urban edge to this garden setting.

Left: Gently curving bleached oak posts offer a vertical contrast to the horizontal sculptural bench designed by Rae Wilkinson.

Homemade vertical garden sculptural elements – why not? Create your own vertical accents using whatever you have to hand; leftover construction timber, empty compact disc cases and stainless steel pipes can all make interesting shapes in the garden.

This garden features vertical accents made from old compact disc boxes, enclosed within a metal frame. Designer Alex Bell first painted the inside of the CD boxes with colours from the garden that he wanted to highlight. Then he built the frames, which range from one to one and half metres tall, using stainless steel edging more usually seen around the edge of household tiles.

Another great idea to create a focal point in a garden is to use existing elements. The trunk of a tree, dead or alive, presents the perfect canvas for paint. If the tree is still alive, be sure to use water-based, non-toxic paint. However, if it's dead, go to town and highlight the natural beauty with a pop of colour.

It can be as simple as painting the trunk of a tree in your garden to create a striking statement. This one, by artist Rod Burns, was painted using organic, water-based paints so that no harm was done to the bark of the tree.

Above: If a tree dies in your garden, don't chop it down immediately. Think of preserving its sculptural form and painting it a striking colour.

Right (top): This tree sculpture is made from wire. Arresting in its simplicity, its short roots and stunted branches bring to mind visions of an apocalyptic landscape.

Right (bottom): While this tree is silhouetted against a fine large living specimen, a contemporary metal cut-out tree sculpture would work well in an urban environment where planting the real thing isn't possible.

Rusted steel triangles add an easy, two dimensional vertical element.

This copper 'energy wave' sculpture takes its cue from jewellery, says designer Andy Sturgeon. "I designed this to provide a dramatic focal point as it weaves its way through the garden into borders and pathways and emerges in the rectangular pool, enlivening the garden without challenging its formality."

This rusted steel support structure is pretty as well as practical.

These copper circles create a semi-transparent barrier, a gently wavy fence.

This wide-leafed rusted steel sculpture acts as focal point, its leaves in stark contrast to the scale of the plants that surround it.

Made from Corten steel, this sculpture called *Window in Time*, draws the eye upwards, but mimics the shape of the clipped topiary below it.

Laser-cut metal panels put a contemporary spin on an urban fence.

These metal panels pack graphic punch. Reminiscent of the ends of stacked logs, they stand in a pool of water, silhouetted against a vibrant blue wall.

These whimsical red birds won't ever be frightened away. Balanced atop a delicate metal frame, they'll float above a sea of cornflowers for endless summer days.

The simple contrast of rusted metal with the colour and texture of driftwood creates a delightfully rustic installation.

Anyone for tea? Don't mind if I do. These whimsical teacup installations bring the Mad Hatter's Tea Party to mind.

Found and recycled objects can make the most whimsical and soulful garden focal points. Strongly rooted in a sense of place, stones, driftwood, bottles or even simple hanging decorations can give just the right lift to a landscape lacking a bit of fun.

Rustic willow hanging balls echo the spiky heads of globe thistles growing below.

These wonderfully rustic stone strings, designed by Rod Burns, lead your eye to the sky.

Perfect for a coastal garden, these contemporary pole sculptures echo west coast North American totem poles. Made from driftwood and reclaimed materials from the beach, this is sculpture made close to home.

Is your garden lacking whimsy and colour? Both are easily solved with simple installations, using colour to create coherence.

Create a garden with international charm with a collection of diverse masks.

Left: Pictures aren't only for your house. Take a tile or two from the mosaic book of Pompeii and hang some exterior art.

Above: This salamander sculpture doubles as a water feature.

Above and right (top and bottom): An insect hotel keeps everyone happy. It provides a place to rest and shelter for happy insects, but also acts as a focal point in a garden with wilder, loose planting.

Mirrored accents amplify the beauty in any garden.

Above: Have some fun with an old ladder – use it as a vertical focal point and a plant stand.

Below: These stacked polished metal balls add just the right amount of shine to a planting scheme of many shades of green. Think of introducing shiny metal into dark garden corners or places where colour is needed.

Part practical, part installation, a display of old watering cans brings a vintage feeling to a corner of the garden.

Above (left): An oversized wire pear makes a statement when backed by architectural plants such as phormiums.

Above (right): Wall art, outside. It's easy to introduce a splash of colour to your terrace garden with these sculptural orange dahlias.

Left: At once contemporary, but with a distinctly rustic feel, these graphic, cheerful stars bring a clapboard wall to life.

Chapter 14

WALL TREATMENTS, FENCES AND HEDGES

Large or small, urban or rural, there's a point at which every garden stops and landscape or a neighbour takes over. Cultivated garden spaces require a perimeter to define them. Larger gardens benefit from definition within, such as screens, dividing walls or hedges, and that's to say nothing of any practical needs, such as enclosing a swimming pool or vegetable garden, or keeping children and animals out.

Walls, fences and hedges offer a sense of enclosure in a garden. By their tall nature, they allow you to create intimate spaces, breaking up a larger landscape into a series of garden rooms. These smaller spaces give you the freedom to play with different styles, different colours and different planting plans. They offer an element of discovery and surprise, they force your eye to appreciate details and linger, rather than viewing a garden in one great sweep.

Think of the sense of mystery and romance of a medieval cloistered garden, or the magic of stepping into a beautifully manicured walled kitchen garden, or one filled with fragrant flowers. Walls create a microclimate due to the warmth they radiate, absorbed during the day from the sun. They also block out the elements to a certain degree, sheltering those plants, vegetables and people lucky enough to be on the inside.

There is no shortage of choice of style and materials for your boundaries. After all, you can build a wall or fence from anything solid – stone, wood, brick, steel, glass, wire – and plant a hedge or screen using any number of plants including willow, box, laurel, bamboo, Thuja, camellia and gardenia.

It's easy to incorporate colour into your hedges by selecting variegated or flowering shrubs and into your fences and walls by the materials you choose – terracotta tiles or vibrant pink painted concrete anyone?

Texture and shape also offer a great opportunity to try something creative. Choose rough-hewn stone, recycled boards, old bricks, ridged tiles, laser-cut panels, stacked timber, shiplap, rounded bamboo canes, Corten steel panels or smooth painted concrete for your fences or walls. Consider a hedge as a blank canvas, waiting to be styled as your own; clipped and neat or whimsically wavy; with topiary animals or framing a gate; cocooning a bench or hiding a piece of sculpture.

There's an old proverb that says, "Good fences make good neighbours." With so much choice, you can't fail to find the perfect solution to your boundary needs and keep every designer's eye happy into the bargain.

Left: A dry stacked Yorkstone panel with a sundial keyhole motif makes an arresting tableau, especially when paired with the loose, wildflower inspired planting in the bed below.

Stone, of every shape, finish and colour is a wonderfully tactile, soft and yet robust material for building a wall. Available in tones of grey, ochre, orange, gray, blue, white, beige and every colour in between, you can choose to dry stack it, layer it, mortar it or hone it, in pieces small or large.

Above: A dry stacked stonewall adds infinite layers of texture and depth to a garden. The palette of blues, greys and white, juxtaposed with timber slats and a modern aesthetic all add up to contemporary harmony.

Left: A dry stacked feature stonewall with a mirror insert provides an interesting counterpoint to a green background.

Left (top) and above: Golden, rough-hewn stone offers a rustic, Mediterranean feel to this tableau, complete with a built-in shelf for a planting trough.

Right (top): Plants love the crevices of walls. Here, moss, tumbling euphorbia and arabis have made a happy home.

Left: Leaving the end of a wall unfinished allows climbing plants to find their way up through the natural steps.

Right: Classic sandstone offers a formal feeling to any garden setting. Here, the wall is successfully paired with a contemporary water feature and drought tolerant planting.

Left and above: This built-in insecthouse is a great idea to increase the visual interest of any wall. In keeping with the dry nature of the stone itself, succulents such as sempervivum, thrive along the top.

Above: The tailored finish to this white stonewall adds to the sophisticated, streamlined vibe of a garden courtyard designed for outdoor living. The space includes a fireplace and edible plants.

Right: Another idea for a dry stacked stonewall is to finish the top of it with stones laid vertically for a varied texture.

Left: At once contemporary and classic, this wall made from a mixed palette of Boral cultured stones, is the perfect backdrop to a contemporary styled seating area. There's even space for a couple of patches of green wall!

Above: This moon gate window in a contemporary vibrant pink wall is especially striking for the contrast it offers with the dark greenery behind it. You can lift your garden or accent wall from ho-hum to spectacular with just a simple coat of paint. Perhaps surprisingly, vibrant colours work well, offering a strong and arresting contrast.

Left: Pink and green is always a winning combination. Here, combined with pleached *Acer campestre* and a mosaic tiled waterfall, the pink walls really pop!

Below: This moon gate window in an old, weather brick wall gives an enchanting glimpse into the garden beyond.

Left: More pink – combined for its effect in contrast with yellow rudbeckias and lime green foliage.

Left (below): The warmth of strong orange is the perfect backdrop to a more muted palette of greens. Small openings spark curiosity and provide a place for small potted succulents.

Right (below): Tex Mex hot! A jewel-toned, two-toned turquoise and burnt orange wall are the perfect backdrop for kniphofia.

Left (top): Mondrian in the garden.

Right (top and bottom): The cool blue of these walls provides a calming backdrop to seating areas.

Left (middle): Deep and distinctly sea-blue, this wall provides a watery backdrop for seaweed-like climbing vines.

Left (bottom): A white wall is like a blank canvas, perfect for decorating any way you like. Here, a graphic pattern of trained ivy creates a green grid in a contemporary garden.

Above: Not for the faint-hearted! This checkerboard pink and purple wall in a Japanese inspired garden will definitely keep the blues away.

Right (top): A purple wall with an alcove provides the perfect place for a quirky clipped conifer and *Armeria maritima* sea thrift.

Right (bottom): These mauve wall strips pick up similar tones found in the stained glass panels and tones of pink and purple in the garden planting.

Below: A pale pink wall with a water feature offers a stunning focal point in a garden with plentiful blue, purple and pink undertones.

Above: An easy and quick-growing way to soften concrete walls is to grow bamboo up them.

Below: White cutout panels impart a distinctly Greek or North African vibe to this cactus garden, while the details in the wall work as a strong counterfoil to the solid, coloured cube planters.

Above: This vivid orange wall is made from three dimensional, weatherproof polyurethane panels, which offer a startling contrast to foliage planted in front.

Below: Modern large-scale mosaic decorative panels.

Above and below: Trompe l'oeil in the garden. A mirror can add deception and depth. Here, mirrors are used in three different ways to give the impression of an opening to another part of the garden.

Right: This feature wall is about texture, shape and colour. With a mirror and bold geometric shapes, echoed in raised and carved panels, this rendered wall offers stimulation for all the senses.

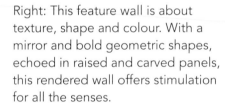

Above and left: Everything about this coastal themed garden conjures days spent at the seaside. From the gently curved wave shaped wall to the waving grasses planted along the top of it, sand dunes, sea grasses and breakers come to mind.

Below: From earth to earth. This wonderfully wavy, burned orange screen is made from terracotta.

Left and above: These cubes with birch trees growing through them are made from Corten steel and stacked to form a semi-transparent screen. On one wall, lumber ends are stacked and cut to different depths to create a chunky wooden wall.

Right: These Corten steel rectangles create a screen-like feeling, guiding the eye to a distant focal point.

Traditionally, when we think of a fence we think of wood. While all of the examples included here are indeed made of wood, only one of them is traditional. The following photographs should inspire you to get creative if you are planning to incorporate a wooden fence or screen into your garden.

Above (left and right): Featuring a cutout panel to allow glimpses of the landscape beyond, this wall is made from timber and timber offcuts, laid to show off their inherent beauty. At once chunky and solid, it is also detailed and delicate.

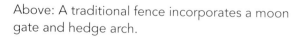

Above: A traditional fence incorporates a moon gate and hedge arch.

Above: These beautiful curved cedar wood arches frame the different parts of this garden, creating garden rooms.

Top (left): If you've got timber odds and ends lying about, this is a great way to use them. Different colours and textures will add plenty of visual interest.

Above: Pine panels can make a contemporary, graphic statement when stained in different colours and laid horizontally.

Bottom (left): This shiplap style fence would be perfect for a beach house or shed. The painted horizontal lines contrast beautifully with the soft shapes of agapanthus.

Below: Just a simple coat of whitewash can give a plain fence a brighter outlook. Add several birdhouses for whimsical wonder.

Above: Woven fencing is a lightweight, more informal option for screens and fences.

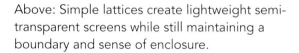

Above: Simple lattices create lightweight semi-transparent screens while still maintaining a boundary and sense of enclosure.

Right: Use wider bamboo poles to create a Japanese inspired fence. Tough, tall and completely renewable, bamboo is a great eco option.

Left (top): Classic and clipped, this buxus hedge is given a dash of whimsy by a line of lollipop balls.

Right (top): Buxus is the classic hedging plant for topiary designs.

Right (bottom): Layered parterre hedging is a great contrast with the soft shapes of santolina and clipped standard ornamental trees.

Left (bottom): Yew is very popular for hedging because it creates a dense, uniform greenery that can be easily kept in shape. Here, formal yew hedges are given a lift by *Photinia 'Red Robin'* clipped topiary lollipops.

Above: Two clipped balls atop a tall formal hedge clearly mark the entry to a different garden 'room'.

Below (left): Dwarf Cypress trees add an exclamation point and a vertical element to a planting scheme that includes low hedges.

Below (right): A magnificent hornbeam hedge with periodic clipped conifer vertical accents.

Left (top): This formal planting of clipped *Laurus nobilis* (laurel) and box hedging, with silver accent planting below is a classically Mediterranean design.

Above: A tall hedging arch offers a glimpse through a window to another part of the garden.

Left middle (top): A window in a mixed yew-beech hedge offers a tantalizing view of meadows beyond.

Left middle (bottom): A window in a taller yew hedge draws the eye upwards, away from the massed planting of alliums below, which mimic the shape of the window.

Left (bottom): A dense hedge makes a perfect arbour.

Above: A hedge offers a deep green sill to a window.

Right (top): This elongated tall yew hedge arch and clipped design introduce a slightly Gothic feel to the landscape.

Right middle (top): A yew hedge is the perfect place to hide a piece of sculpture.

Right middle (bottom): The simple shape of this Japanese-inspired, cloud pruned yew hedge is deceptive. This kind of pruning and training can take a very long time.

Right (bottom): A hedge need not be just one texture or colour. Here, mixing plants creates a tapestry effect.

Above (top): Neat layers of clipped hedges are softened by the abundant flowering roses.

Above (middle): A stone terrace and tall curved hedge offer the perfect spot for this handsome semi-circular bench.

Above (bottom): The deep glossy green leaves and jaunty red flowers of a camellia hedge make a great contrast with the small leaved, bright green hedge below.

Above (top): A tall backed seat neatly positioned in a clipped recess in a dense hedge lifts the eye to enjoy the rolling landscape beyond.

Above (bottom): Vibrant red highlights pop from this photinia hedge.

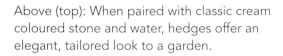

Above (top): When paired with classic cream coloured stone and water, hedges offer an elegant, tailored look to a garden.

Above (bottom): A dense hedge is the perfect foil to a stone and rusted metal water feature.

Right: These striking tall, square lollipop trees are pleached hornbeam.

Left (top): Pleached hornbeams create the feeling of intimacy in this circular gravel garden, while still allowing views between the trunks.

Right (top): An avenue of pleached hornbeams.

Right (bottom): Pleached hornbeams in autumn with a splendid orange glow.

Left (bottom): For an informal hedge structure, choose tall grass, hebe and perovskia.

Above (top): A plain hedge backdrop focuses the eye on a natural stone envelope water feature

Above: A hawthorn hedge is a dense, dark backdrop for a rusted steel water panel.

Left: Layered hedging techniques create a clean-lined, classic look for a courtyard space.

Chapter 15

RECYCLING FOR VERTICAL ELEMENTS

There is so much potential for gardening in many of the day-to-day objects that society throws away. A quick glance around any construction site will reveal metal and plastic pipes, ductwork, empty glass containers, wood offcuts of all shapes and sizes, empty drums and plenty of wire. All of these things can be re-purposed into budget do-it-yourself ideas to create vertical accents in your own garden. Throw in a lick of paint and a dash of inspiration and you'll have something unique, cheap and a great conversation piece.

Left (top): This earthy, rustic installation incorporates a water feature and an insect hotel. Built using reclaimed timber and rusted aluminium cans, small sticks and bamboo offer shelter for insects and bees inside the cans.

Left (bottom) and below: This installation embodies cottage garden upcycling. Reclaimed orange metal panels serve as the backdrop to a water feature using the green spouts from a combine harvester, which in turn water the plants in the container below. A small living roof garden on the adjacent shed only augments the green credentials of this scheme.

Left (top): This whimsical garden screen was created from recycled and found objects. The basic shape relies on the base of cut steel drums on shelves, subsequently filled with laser filigree cut outs, curled ivy, bicycle spokes and found objects to create insect habitats.

Above: Nature builds her own barriers. Here, large reclaimed timber vertical posts have been interspersed with log offcuts to create a rustic fence.

Left middle (top): This is a log pile in its simplest form but one that serves many purposes – as fence, as decorative wooden wall and as a habitat for small animals such as fieldmice and birds.

Left middle (bottom): This green oak log fence was built using 20cm pieces of wood, stacked between tall, square cut posts. Built in stacked layers, this cosy corner is eye catching because of the many different diameters of logs used which creates a mosaic-like pattern. It's also a habitat for wildlife, happy to hide in all the nooks and crannies.

Left (bottom): This is a very simple, but nonetheless fun idea to add a shot of whimsy to an old fence. Cover the tops of the posts with tiny terracotta pots.

Left (top): This tableau is easy to make out of an old frame, some aged terracotta pots and wire. Add some ivy – but don't let it get out of control – and you've created a living picture.

Above: Don't throw away that broken ladder! Salvage the best of it to create a stand to tidy away garden tools.

Left (bottom): Shape and texture are two valuable tools in a gardener's box. Here, drilled out logs and bamboo sticks are combined with succulents to create an eye-catching installation that can be installed on a fence or atop a wall.

This hyper-contemporary, space age garden dividing screen was created using aluminium pipes. Connected into a sinuous elongated snake shape, pipes were filled with a perlite soil mix and holes cut out for plants such as succulents, lobelia, pansies and herbs. Juxtaposed with a display of colourful painted planter pots, there's plenty of visual interest in this garden.

Who says you have to hide a garden shed? Make the most of it by using reclaimed lumber and then painting it in vibrant stripes. Strong colours work well in climates with hot sun, while you should choose paler colours where the light and heat is more temperate.

Never let a good palette go to waste. Transform them into planting racks with a simple coat of paint and fill with herbs.

Old oil drums have been cut, leaving a decorative edge, then etched, before they were filled with overflowing herbs and vegetables.

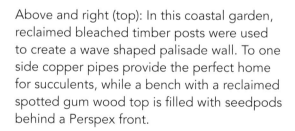

Above and right (top): In this coastal garden, reclaimed bleached timber posts were used to create a wave shaped palisade wall. To one side copper pipes provide the perfect home for succulents, while a bench with a reclaimed spotted gum wood top is filled with seedpods behind a Perspex front.

Right (bottom): In an abundant vegetable garden, this tomato wall was created using recycled plastic grids of about 5 cm deep, attached to a sheet of plywood. Planted from tiny plugs and laid horizontally until established, the tomato sheets were then erected vertically against posts and watered using a drip system.

Above: Here's a really simple, decorative use for old bedsprings – as a garden screen or climbing support for vegetables. They're the perfect weight to create a lightweight, semi-transparent screen for climbing plants or support structure for peas, cucumbers and other vegetable garden climbers.

Below (left): In another life, this metal ring might be used as a cattle or horse feeder, to contain a huge round bale of hay. But here it serves as a contemporary entryway to a garden, fabulously framing views beyond.

Below (right): What could be simpler than rustic, not quite straight tree offcuts to line a pathway and offer support for growing vegetables such as sweetcorn and beans?

Above: A beachcomber's collage includes an outdoor clock, mounted to great effect on a painted wall.

Right (top and bottom): This is a fun and easy project for children: Create their own bottle planters. Simply take a large, empty plastic pop bottle, cut a hole in one side for your flower and fill with planting mix. Add a cheerful flower of your child's choice and suspend using string. Water regularly.

Chapter 16

RAISED AND TERRACED BEDS

As urban density has increased and the cost of green space in cities has become out of this world, urban planners have been looking to disused land to create green space. Since 1993, three expansive elevated parks have been built atop disused railway lines in Paris, New York City and Chicago. They are the ultimate raised flowerbeds on a grand scale.

La Promenade Plantée opened in Paris in 1993. Built along the former tracks of the Vincennes railway line to the east of the Bastille, at its western end it travels along the Viaduc des Arts some 10-metres in the air, before descending to ground level at its eastern end, near the Boulevard Péréphérique. The 4.7 km elevated park was the only elevated park in the world until 2009 when the High Line, an urban green space designed along similar ideas, opened on the west side of Manhattan.

The High Line uses the old West Side rail line and stretches for 2.33 kilometres. It features predominantly rugged meadow plants, grasses and Native American species, as well as rolling benches and pebble dash concrete walkways. The park attracts five million visitors annually. In Chicago, the 4.34 kilometre long Bloomingdale Trail opened in June 2015. It's another elevated linear park, built along disused rail lines that offers green space in the heart of an urban environment.
While these are examples of public infrastructure projects on a huge scale, they illustrate the interest in and attraction of raised and terraced green space.

You can decrease the scale a hundredfold and create your own raised and terraced garden spaces at home. In fact, differences in elevation in your garden can offer great opportunity for building terraces and raised flowerbeds; for creating different garden 'rooms'; for minimising damage by pests; for incorporating plants of wildly varying heights; and for gardening at knee or waist height – better for your back and knees!

Left (top and bottom): Timber facades grace raised beds of several levels that include clipped buxus spheres, Geum, ferns, grasses and *Camassia leichtlinii 'Plena Alba'*.

Above: These oversized rendered planters impart a desert vibe to planting that includes red and yellow coloured flowers such as Kniphofia, agave, marigolds, Tagetes and pumpkins.

Below: These raised brick beds with a wide stone sill for sitting and gardening, create the perfect spot to plant a cottage garden. Flowers include verbascum, lychnis, geraniums, *Alchemilla mollis*, *Salvia nemorosa 'Sensation Rose'* and lavender.

Left (top): This simple brick raised bed uses trailing ivy and nasturtiums to soften the edge of the bricks.

Left (middle): This white walled raised bed hits the mark on several levels. It not only offers a contemporary, clean ambiance to the garden, but the timber top to the walls is both beautiful for use as a bench and the perfect place to sit to do some weeding. Plants include variegated hebe, achillea and salvia.

Left (bottom): This raised vegetable garden made from reclaimed scaffold boards gets playful with colour to highlight the chard, sage, basil and carrots planted within.

Above: A narrow area alongside a house benefits from raised beds with rendered walls, leaving plenty of space for a tidy pathway and a garden overflowing with sedum, grasses, Penstemon and salvia.

Left (top) and above: While this bed is only slightly raised – just enough to keep the gravel out of the ground – it also incorporates other vertical elements such as espaliered pear and apple trees, and a dwarf conifer.

Left (bottom) and below: These deep raised beds – mini potagers and flowers for a cutting garden - are built to different heights for sitting or standing gardening. Plants include salad leaves, cabbage, strawberries, beans, violas, thyme, chard and cosmos.

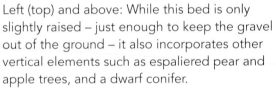

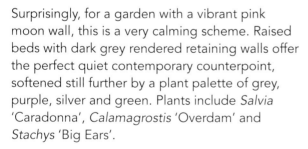

Surprisingly, for a garden with a vibrant pink moon wall, this is a very calming scheme. Raised beds with dark grey rendered retaining walls offer the perfect quiet contemporary counterpoint, softened still further by a plant palette of grey, purple, silver and green. Plants include *Salvia* 'Caradonna', *Calamagrostis* 'Overdam' and *Stachys* 'Big Ears'.

The choice of red flowers and a vibrant orange perimeter wall with Aboriginal painting highlight the colours of a raised flower bed wall made from stacked sandstone pavers.

Left: Stepped rugged timber retaining walls offer a place to sit and a backdrop of yucca, phormium and miscanthus.

Above: This garden offers classical elegance in a muted palette of green, pale cream sandstone and dark grey. While the planting and colour is limited, the many different levels offer visual interest in this serene garden.

Below: With tumbling roses and plenty of pretty pots, a series of raised beds lead one to the top of this hillside cottage garden.

Above: Trailing ivy softens the walls of these raised beds, planted for spring with tulips, alium and bluebells.

Right (top): It's a simple idea to add a couple of pots to a terrace wall to soften the edges.

Right (bottom): The scale of the stone used for the raised bed and the backdrop wall draw the viewer's eye upwards in this garden. The smaller pieces of stone used for the raised bed retaining wall focus the eye on the drought tolerant planting in the bed, while the massive pieces used behind serve as the perfect neutral backdrop.

Below: A simple plank is all it takes to make a petty place to sit on the wall of a raised bed.

For an expansive space, timber retaining walls are more cost effective and generally easier to install. Here, the terraces make a happy home for guara, achillea, salvia, *Verbena bonariensis*, geraniums, penstemon, *Stipa tenuissima* and Echinacea.

Above: This terraced garden uses many clever tricks to lead your eye upwards. A natural progression of steps lead to a pergola, which in turn leads the eye to vibrant purple planting of lavender, abundant roses and a soft brick wall at the back of the garden.

Left: Here's a terraced garden with a distinctly Mediterranean feel. Golden gravel, contrasts with the deep green of conifers, ceanothus, box and rosemary.

Turn your retaining walls into an opportunity for an opulent display. There are plenty of plants that will thrive growing in the crevices of a wall, offering a tumbling, soft pillow of colour and texture. Here, frothy massed aubretia and *Phlox subulata* cascade over stone walls, accompanied by tulips for a spring show. Later, tufty mounds of fragrant lavender pick up the purple colour scheme through summer.

Use a slope in your garden to create a terraced water feature with damp-loving plants.

Use your slope as nature would, by creating a water feature that looks like it was always there.

Succulents and plants that tumble and drape, such as rosemary, are happy to colonise a wall.

Chapter 17

TALL TREES AND ACCENT PLANTS

Is there anything more awe-inspiring than standing beneath a magnificent, huge old-growth tree and looking up through its branches and leaves, through dappled sunlight and a canopy of green, to darting triangles of blue sky above? Or even a stand of silvery silver birch trees, trembling in the breeze? Trees bring landscapes to life. A landscape without trees is little more than a decorated field, no matter how many pretty plants you add. As soon as you add trees, you add height, depth and layering to your landscape.

Trees add architectural interest and a sense of structure, but only if you choose the right tree for the right spot. Most important, is to consider what your tree will look like in 20 years' time. You must choose trees that will ultimately be the right scale for the size of your garden. Then consider the shape you hope to achieve – both in summer with leaves and the skeletal form in winter with none, if it's a deciduous tree – and any colour it might offer. Consider the golden, red and orange glow of maples in autumn and the intense, lime green of an early spring birch. Consider any flowers that your tree might produce – horse chestnuts, magnolia, cherry trees and catalpa come to mind for their spectacular spring flowers – or any berries at the other end of the season. All of these things add value and interest to the tree you choose.

You can choose to plant trees in single splendid specimens, or in copses; in layers of height, or clipped into shapes; in avenues or as focal points to create rhythm through your garden.

You should also consider how the tree you choose works with other garden plants. Some, such as copper beech and many conifers, simply make it hard to grow anything at all under their canopies, as the ground is generally dry and often shady.

Quite apart from the aesthetic benefits, trees also offer hugely positive environmental benefits such as shade in hot climates and barriers against cold winter winds. They filter water and air to reduce soil erosion and control run-off, and just one mature tree can clean about 330lbs. of carbon dioxide from the air annually. Trees have also been shown to reduce stress.

This loose copse of silver birch naturally draws the eye upwards, as the striped lawn before it draws the eye horizontally.

The bark of the silver birch is stunning in summer, but in winter, they can become green and covered with algae. A quick wash with a soft brush and some warm water will reveal the stunning bright bark underneath.

A birch glade offers a gentle, dappled shade and the perfect environment for spring flowers such as daffodils, wood anemone and hellebores.

Three silver birch trees add a lightweight vertical element to a flowerbed and a pretty autumn contrast with a persicaria ground cover.

The gently angled trunks of a mature birch specimen can offer the perfect place for a tree house platform and shade canopy.

A small copse of birch adds a vertical element in a design that includes a sculpture for a strong focal point and loose, natural planting.

The stones underneath pick up the soft grey tones of the foliage of this Ilex specimen tree, while the planting of massed aquilegia mirrors the soft mounding shape of the canopy.

An arching *Malus* 'Golden Hornet' anchors an alfresco dining area, as well as offering shade.

A fine example of a mature *Acer griseum* with its characteristic peeling bark, juxtaposed with a neatly clipped box hedge at its foot.

Acer griseum, more commonly known as the Paperbark Maple, offers intriguing coppery bark peelings and a statuesque shape in winter.

These magnificent Acer produce splendid colours in autumn, from golden yellow to vibrant red. Growing in their own beds, they are fertilised by their own falling leaves, which create a natural mulch.

The peeling bark of *Acer griseum* adds textural interest to spring planting when contrasted with hellebores, berberis, tulips and carex grass.

A weeping prunus looks pretty when under planted with soft spring colours.

Left and above: The repeated use of tall, elegant *Betula albosinensis* 'Fascination' with their bronze bark creates a rhythmic, contemporary feel when juxtaposed with the rusted curved steel panels in this garden. Note how the trees cast pretty shadows on the wall.

Left: With its generous bunches of bright pink flowers, a flowering cherry tree gives a lift to any spring garden.

Below: The pure white blossoms of a flowering cherry tree create a spectacular show when under planted with plentiful spring tulips.

The deep pink flowers of magnolia, which fade through pale pink to nearly white, create a stunning display when paired with poppies.

A *Prunus serrula* makes a pretty sculptural shape to anchor a bench.

A Japanese acer offers a mid-level layer of structure and dappled shade to plants such as hosta, primulas and ferns planted underneath.

The vibrant red of a maple contrasts nicely with the still-green leaves of hosta in autumn.

You can use a small copse of trees to break up an expanse of green. Here, elegant *Sorbus aria* trees are planted in a circle, creating their own little tree feature.

Above (top): *Prunus Serrula* bark detail

Above: If you find you have a tree in a courtyard, think of using containers around its base to add different layers of interest.

Left: A close-up of *Acer griseum's* copper-toned, peeling bark.

Above: A very effective way to lead the eye from one point to another is to plant an avenue of repeated trees.

Note: Not every tree is amenable to clipping, but there are some tried and true varieties that respond well to decorative trimming, such as lollipop, pyramid, column and cone shapes, all of which focus your attention and lead your eye skywards.

Right (top and middle): Acers, holly and variegated buxus make cheerful lollipop trees that add a touch of manicured whimsy to the garden.

Right (bottom): Trimmed trees look particularly sculptural as part of a parterre.

Left (above and middle): The Hornbeam is a very adaptable tree, which can be clipped to lollipop or column shapes, or pleached to form a tree screen.

Above: This avenue of square clipped linden trees with square clipped box at their feet creates a pleasing symmetry and draws the eye to a distant point.

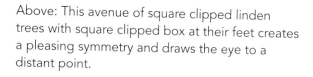

Left (below) and below: Cloud pruning is a Japanese method of training trees and shrubs into shapes that resemble cartoon clouds. There are many varieties of trees, shrubs and hedging that will adapt to this form of pruning. Here, buxus, a conifer and holly show what can be achieved.

Left: The silvery undersides of the leaves of a weeping pear make the perfect companion for soft mounds of santolina planted underneath.

A tree seat is the perfect way to make a feature of a specimen tree. It offers a shady spot to rest, but also an anchor for the bench, to admire other parts of the garden.

Above (top): Large trees create shade and sometimes dry conditions, which make it difficult to grow many plants underneath. Here, clivia is a good solution.

Above (bottom): One way to highlight a feature tree is to create a lush garden around it to draw the eye. Here, an *Acer pseudoplatanus* 'Prinz Handjery' is offset by a flowerbed of a slightly larger diameter than its canopy, planted with soft grasses, dahlias, arctotis and Eucomis pineapple lilies.

Above (top): A neatly clipped box hedge at the foot of a tree is one way to emphasise the vertical nature of the tree.

Above (bottom): A whimsical topiary forest of miniature trees offers an amusing contrast to the soft, moving leaves of the silver birch planted above.

Above: A contemporary way to include a tree in your outdoor living area is to build a floating deck around it. This will give the tree space to continue to grow.

Right (top): Just because you live in an apartment doesn't mean you shouldn't have trees. Think of planting smaller varieties in larger planters to create a green screen.

Below: Here, a tree is used as the support structure to grow pumpkins.

Right (bottom): The beautiful, grainy bark of a tree is the perfect place to site a carving, anchor a sculpture and hang a flowering basket.

Left (top): Clipped pyramid yew conifers create a graphic exclamation point in any garden and bring Egypt to mind.

Left (middle): Yews live for a very long time. In this photograph they have been clipped and stand like soldiers along a wall, offering a vertical element to the strongly horizontal hard landscaping features of the walls and stonework.

Above: Soften the edges of a pyramid and you have a cone shaped conifer. Here, a pair of cone conifers stand sentinel to an entrance to a walled garden.

Left (bottom) and below: Topiary shapes add vertical points of interest and can be clipped to any shape that fits your garden or appeals to your sense of humour.

Left: An appealing mix of topiary shapes line a driveway.

Above: Standard fruit trees offer a mid-level accent in a garden with low to the ground plantings.

Bottom (left): A lollipop bay tree contrasts with a square clipped box hedge below.

Bottom (middle): Tall and slim dwarf conifers by a water feature lead the eye to the sky.

Bottom (right): Tall trees clipped to lollipop shapes contrast with short topiary shrubs to make a statement entrance.

Above: Standard photinias show their wonderful green and red colours and add a vertical element to a flowerbed.

Above: These copper beech cones add a splash of colour and an interesting shape on a small scale.

Below: Tree ferns are a great way to introduce a tropical vibe to your garden. Since there are upwards of one thousand different species, you're sure to be able to find one of the perfect size.

Below: Bamboo makes a fast-growing and attractive vertical accent. It can be used to grow a screen or fence, as a focal point, as a backdrop and even to create the feeling of an avenue.

Below: Another plant that can create a show-stopping focal point is phormium. They too have sword-shaped leaves and can range in colour from dark burgundy to pale green and pink.

Above: The Yucca is a genus of shrubs and trees, which typically share tough, sword-shaped leaves and some of which grow into extraordinary shapes that can create arresting focal points in a garden.

Above: This picture shows the importance of building layers through your garden. Here, progressively taller plants create a textured, lush and full picture, which is interesting and pretty.

Above: Giant sunflowers are a great way to introduce height to any garden. They can be used as screens between neighbours or simply as a vertical accent at the back of a garden bed. Often planted in vegetable gardens as they are fast-growing from seed, they add a cheerful element wherever they're found.

Above: The delicate, swaying spires of delphinium, foxgloves and lupins make excellent transition plants. Their mid-level height bridges the gap between ground cover and many smaller perennial plants, but does not interfere with trees. Their spike-like spires are often seen in informal cottage gardens and in flowerbeds where vertical accents are needed

PLANT LISTS

Chapter 1 - Page 8 &11 - Athenaeum Hotel
Agapanthus Africans
Acanthus mollis
Beschorneria yuccoides
Berberis 'Orange King'
Chamaecyparis pisifera
Choisya ternata
Delosperma cooperi
Dicksonia antarctica
Erysimum 'Bowles Mauve'
Erigeron
Fatsia japonica
Fuchsia magellanica
Geranium sanguineum
Gypsophila repens
Hemerocallis
Helleborus foetidus
Heptacodium miconiodes
Iris confusa
Jasminum officinale
Kniphofia
Leycesteria formosa
 Lonicera 'Graham Thomas' -
Mimulus
 Mahonia japonica
 Nandina domestica
 Narcissus
 Ophiopogon nigrescens
Pittosporum tobira
Pachysandra terminalis
Raphiolepsis indica
 Rosmarinus prostratus
Senecio greyi
Sarcococca hookeriana
Tricyrtris formosana
Ugni
Viburnum davidii
Vinca minor
Woodwardia radicans
Yucca filamentosa

Chapter 2 – page 14 & 15 – Heather garden
Heathers in wall
Erica carnea 'Challenger', 'Isabell' and 'Wintersonne'
Erica x darleyensis 'Furzey', 'J.W. Porter', 'Katia', 'Kramer's Rote', 'Lucie', 'White Perfection', 'White Spring Surprise' and 'Winter surprise'

In garden:-
Calluna vulgaris 'Forest Fire', 'Silver Fox' and 'Tib'
Daboecia cantabrica f.alba

Daboecia cantabrica 'April Fool', 'Amelie', 'Atropurpurea', 'Tinkerbelle' and 'Waley's Red'
Daboecia cantabria f. blumii 'White Blum'
Erica ciliaris 'Bretagne', 'David McClintock' and 'Globosa'
Erica cinerea 'Joyce Burfitt', 'My Love' and 'Vivienne Patricia'
Erica mackayanna 'Errigal Dusk'
Erica mackayanna f. eburnean 'Shining Light'
Erica x stuartii 'Irish Lemon'
Erica tetralix 'Alba Mollis', 'Con Underwood'
Erica tetralix f. stellata 'Pink Star'
Erica tetralix 'Riko'
Erica x watsonii 'Mary' and 'Pink Pacific'

(if room to include or can shorten Jess)
Ferns:
Blechnum spicant
Epimedium grandiflorum 'Lilafee'
Rodgersia 'Herkules'
Grasses / Architectural plants:
Astelia chathamica 'Silver Spear'
Miscanthus sinensis 'Gracillimus'
Ophiopogon planiscapus 'Nigrescens'
Herbaceous:
Agastache rugosa 'Black Adder'
Centaura pulchra 'Major'
Echinecea angustifolia
Geranium 'Rozanne'
Lavandula angustifolia 'Hidcote'
Salvia nemorosa 'Caradonna'
Sanguisorba officinalis 'Arnhem'
Verbena bonariensis
Veronicastrum virginicum 'Fascination'
Shade plants:
Asplenium scolopendrum
Epimedium grandiflorum 'Lilafee'
Hosta 'Francee'
Shrubs:
Pinus mugo
Sambucus nigra 'Black Lace'
Viburnum opulus
Viburnum tinus 'Purpurea'
Trees:
Parrotia persica

Page 16 & 17 – Buddha garden
Heuchera 'Purple Palace' & 'Green Spice'
ferns Asplenium Polystichum Pachysandra
Geranium macrorrhizum
Hebe pinguifolia
Vinca minor

Page18 – Monaco garden
Carpobrotus edulis
Osteospermum 'Sunbrella Salmon'

Lampranthus spectabilis
Lavandula
Yucca
Olive trees
Aloe
Geums
Caratonia siliqua

Page 19 – contemporary courtyard
Lamium maculatum
Epimedium x rubrum
Hosta 'Green Edger'
Lamium 'Beacon Silver'
Tiarella 'Ninja'
Adiantum pedatum
Polypodium vulgare

Page 20 – courtyard panel
living wall
Vinca minor atropurpurea
Vinca minor 'Gertrude Jekyll'
Polypodium vulgare
Heuchera 'Obsidian
In garden
Digitalis 'Camelot White'
Lupinus 'Gallery White'
Betula utilis jacquemontii
Pennisetum orientalis 'Tall Tails'
Stipa tenuissima

Page 21 – white courtyard
Acorus gramineus 'Ogon'
Geranium mac. 'White Ness/Alba'
Fuchsia mag. 'Thompsonii'
Euphorbia amyg. 'Robbiae'
Liriope muscari 'Big Blue'
Pellaea falcata
Polystichum polyblefarum
Pachysandra 'Green Carpet'
Polystichum tsus-simense
Hedera helix
Waldsteinia ternate

Page 23 – outdoor room
Polystichum tsussimense
Asplenium scolopendrium
Carex evergold/ morrowii
Hosta Devon green
Polypodium vulgare
Cyrtomium fortunei
Asarum Europ.
Euphorbia Amygdaloides
Pachysandra terminalis

Page 24 right
Bergenia
Tiarella
Primula
Luzula
Vinca
Dryopteris
Polypodium
Asplenium

Page 25
Tradescantia zebrina
Asplenium antiquum
Chlorophytum comosum 'Ocean'
Tillandsia usneoides
Philodendron scandens
Peperomia angulata
Syngonium red and pink
Syngonium 'Pixie'
Sellaginella

Page 26 & 27
Liriope muscari
Ardisia japonica
Nephrolepis exaltata 'Teddy Junior'
Brachyscome iberidifolia 'Marius Blue'
Pachysandra axillaris 'Greeb Sheen'
Pachysandra terminalis
Ophiopogon japonicas
Hedera helix 'Pittsburgh'
Pyrrosia lingua
Crytomium falcatum '
Pteris nipponica 'W.C. Shieh'
Acorus gramineus 'Ougon'
Syngonium podophyllum 'White Butterfly'
Heuchera 'Strawberry Swirl'
Ipomoea batatas 'Sweetheart Light Green'

Chapter 3 - Page 31 top right
Hakonechloa macra
Epimedium youngianum
Euphorbia cyparisus 'Fein's ruby'
Hosta lancifolia
Dicentra 'Bachannal'
Saxifraga x urbium
Heuchera 'Mahogany'

Page 32 top – beach house
Vinca major 'Variegata'
Carex elata 'Aurea'
Polypodium vulgare
Saracococca confusa
Euonymus
Bergenia cordifolia
Liriope muscari

Helchrysum
Euphorbia robbiaea
Helleborus orientalis
Lamium beacon silver
Hosta halcyon
Polystichum setiferum
Hedera helix 'Green Ripple'
Galium odorata
Pennisetum alopecuroides
Erysimum 'Bowles's Mauve'

Page 32 bottom
Skimmia japonica 'Rubella'
Viola tri-colour
Erigeron karvinskianus
Polypodium vulgare
Bergenia cordifolia
Luzula nivea
Luzula sylvatica
Pelargonium pelatum

Page 33 bottom right
Organium vulgare
Calamintha species
Speedwells veronica
Eryngium
Echinops
Papaver rhoeas
Lamium
Raspberry
Lungwort (pulmonaria species)
Broom
Ferns

Page 34 top
Erysimum 'Bowles's Mauve'
Heuchera 'Plum Pudding',
Acorus 'Ogon'
Pachysandra terminalis
Liriope muscari
Pelargonium
Euphorbia robbiae

Page 35 top and left
Stipa 'Horse tails'
Heuchera 'Plum Pudding'
Erysimum 'Bowles's Mauve'
Acorus 'Pgon'
Agapanthus 'Snowflake'

Page 35 bottom right
Crytomium falcatum
Blechnum penna-marina
Polystichum 'Divisilobum'
Polystichum Braunii

Polypodium vulgare
Asplenium scolopendrium 'Critatum'
Helleborus x hrbridus
Epimedium x perralchichum 'Frohnleiten'
Vinca minor 'Variegata'

Page 36 & 37 - Lightwell
Heuchera 'Stormy Seas'
Heuchera 'Beauty Colour'
Carex Foliosissima 'Irish Green'
Euphorbia purpurea
Sarcococca hookeriana
Polystichum polyblefarum
Cyrtomium falcatum
Asplenium scolopendrium
Euphorbia 'Humpty Dumpty'
Veronica penduncularis 'Georgia Blue'
Pachysandra terminalis
Hedera 'Helix Wonder'

Chapter 4 - Page 6 & 40 – B&Q – Edible high-rise
Beta vulgaris 'Rhubard Chard'
Brassica rapa var. purpurea
Capsicum Denver F1
Capiscum Apache F1
Calendula officinalis
Solanum melongena Bonice F1
Lycospersicon Tumbler F1
Phaseolus Hestia
Tropaeolum majus 'Tom Thumb mixed'
Chamaemelum nobile
Origanum vulgare 'Nanum'
Origanum vulgare 'Thumbles Variety'
Thymus vulgaris 'Compactus'
Thymus 'Jekka'
Thymus 'Silver Queen'

Page 41 – Freshly prepped
Baby leaves 'Bulls Blood' , 'Red cos lettuce' ,'Romano Rossa'
Biona Ricciolina
 Endive 'Romanesco
Lettuce' Nymans'
Lollo rosso
Mizuna
Pak Choi 'Red Lady'
Red Veined Sorrel
Spinach 'Fiorano F1'

Page 42 – Citrus courtyard
specimen Lemon Tree
specimen Peach trees,'Peregrine'
Apple 'Stepovers', 'Red Falstaff' and 'Scrumptious'
Achillea 'Sumerwine' & 'Terracotta'

Vertical Planted Wall Capsicum chillies and small peppers,
tumbling tomatoes
Thymus (3 varities)
Mentha

Page 43 – eat landscape
Beta vulgaris subsp. cicla 'Ruby Chard'
Salvia officinalis 'Purpurascens'
Beta vulgaris 'Boltardy' Beetroot
Brassic oleracea var acephala
'Redbor' Kale
Brassica napus var napobrassica
'Purple Top Milan' Turnip
Brassica oleracea gongolydes
'Lanro' Kohlrabi
Brassica oleracea var acephala 'Nero
di Toscana Precoce' Kale
Brassica oleracea var capitata
'Greyhound' Cabbage
Brassica oleracea var gongolydes
'Delicacy Purple' Kohlrabi
Daucus carota 'Flyaway' Carrot
Kadu / Afghanistan Pumpkin
Malva sp. Panirak/Mallow
Praecitrullus fistulosus Indian round
gourd
Trigonella foenum-graecum
Fenugreek

Page 44 & 45 – Potential Feast
Achillea ageratum
Angelica archangelica
Borage officinalis
Chamaemelam nobile 'Treneague'
Foeniculum vulgare 'Purpureum'
Mentha x piperita f.Citrala 'Chocolate'
Salvia officinalis 'Incterina'
Salvia officinalis 'Purpurescens
Aubergine
Beetroot
Broad Bean
Curly Kale
Dwarf Bean
'Lollo Rosso' lettuce
Purple cabbage
Purple podded pea
Rhubarb chard
Runner bean
Tomato 'Tumbling Tom'
Nasturtium 'Velvet Queen'
Sunflower 'Earthwalker'

Chapter 5 - Page 52 – Contoured Stripes
Ajuga reptens 'Bronze Beauty'
Ajuga reptens 'Chocolate Chip'
Euonymus fortunei 'Kewensis'
Vinca minor Alba
Waldsteinia ternate
Helleborus niger
Heuchera 'Silver Scroll'
Heuchera 'Bronze Wave'
Heucherella 'Kimono'
Heucherella 'Stoplight'
Tellima grandiflora
Euphorbia amyg. 'Robbiae'
Asplenium scolupendrium
Cyrtomium fortune
Polystichum braunii
Acorus gramineus 'Variegata'
Carex comens 'Small Red'
Carex testacea
Carex 'Ice Dance'
Deschampsia caespitose
Liriope muscari 'Silver Sceptre'
Ophiopogon japonica

Chapter 6 – page 64 & 66
Crassula undulatifolia
Crassula plathyphylla
Haworthia limifolia (Fairy washboard)
Echeveria 'Morning Beauty'
Echeveria glauca
Echeveria 'Lemon and Lime'
Rhipsalis spp.
Kalanchoe 'flapjack'
Graptoveria
Oscularia deltóides
Senecio mandraliscae
Sedum burrito
Sedum morganianum
Euphorbia spp.
Graptopetalum
Aloe humilis
Schlumbergera.
Senecio rowleyanus
Aeonium decorum 'Kiwi'
Ceropegia woodii

Page 67
Adiantum venustrum
Hakenochloa
Small leaved Ivy Helxine
Solleirolli
Mouse eared hosta
Stolonifera

ACKNOWLEDGEMENTS

The author, Hattie Klotz, and photographer, Leigh Clapp, would like to thank the following for their assistance or allowing their gardens to be photographed

*P.11: *Humans and Nature: How Knowing and Experiencing Nature Affect Well-Being*, Annual Review of Environment and Resources.

Companies and systems
Biotecture, UK: 4, 5, 12, 13 right, 18, 20, 24 right, 36, 37, 41, 47, 53 left, 71, 75, 88
Scotscape, UK: 16, 17, 23, 28, 29, 31 bottom, 32 bottom, 33 bottom, 34 top, 35 top and left, 70, 76, 90
ANS Global, UK: 16, 17, 19, 24 left, 32 left and right, 35 bottom, 42, 43, 46 right, 55 bottom left, 58, 77, 91 left
Vertology, UK: 21, 31 left, 34 bottom, 72, 73, 74
Treebox, UK: 22, 54 left,
Uniseal, Singapore: 25
ELT, USA: 31 right
Vertiflora, UK: 33 top
Burgon and Ball: 46 left, 49 left, 56, 57 images courtesy of Burgon & Ball
Humko Bled, Slovenia: 55 top
VertiGarden, UK: 14, 15, 39 left, 44, 45
Atlantis Gro-Wall, Aust: 64, 66
Landtech Soils, Ireland: 66, 67
Pixel-Garden, UK: 65 left, 68, 69
The Royal Horticultural Society, for access to RHS gardens and RHS shows
The National Gardens Scheme, UK, for access to gardens

Designers
Patrick Blanc: 8, 11
William Quarmby, UK: 14, 15
Philip Nixon, UK: 16, 17
Sarah Eberle, UK: 12, 13 right, 18
Kate Gould, UK: 19, 24 left, 35 bottom, 55 bottom left, 160 bottom, 198 top right
Claire Moreno, Wendy von Buren, Amy Robertson, UK: 20
Belderbos Landscapes, UK: 21
Matthew Childs, UK: 22, 203 top left
Arit Anderson, UK: 23
Patrick Collins, UK: 6, 24 right, 39, 40,
John Tan & Raymond Toh, Singapore: 25,
Fuminari Todaka, Japan: 13 left, 26, 27
Cameron Landscapes, UK: 30
Ian Dexter, UK: 31 right
LDC Gardens, UK: 31 left
Imogen Cox, UK: 33 top
Kingsbury Design, UK: 37
Patricia Fox, UK: 38, 41, 46 right, 47
Mandy Buckland, UK: 42
Emily Ross, UK: 43

Raine Clarke-Willis and Fiona Godman-Dorington, UK: 39 left, 44, 45, 151 bottom right, 165 top right
Mike Harvey, UK: 49, 50
Peter Reader, UK: 51
Paul Hensey, UK: 49, 52, 170 top
Mark Gregory, UK: 53 left
Esra Parr, UK: 54 left
DeakinLock, UK: 54 right
Tomaz Bavdez, UK: 55 top
Caroline E. Butler, UK: 55 bottom right
Plants in Space, UK: 58, 120 bottom left
Marian Boswall, UK: 59-63, 207 top left and middle
Carmel Quill, Aust: 64, 66
Jo Carter, UK: 131 bottom middle
Jennifer Gayler, UK: 132
Arne Maynard, UK: 139 left, 141 top
sculptor Rudi Jass, Aust.: 139 right
John Warland, UK: 142 bottom
Kerianne Mulqueen, UK: 146 top
Paul Stone, UK: 147 top, 189 bottom right
Rae Wilkinson, UK: 147 bottom
Alex Bell, UK: 148 left
artist Rod Burns, UK: 148 right, 153 top right, 177 left, right middle
Andy Sturgeon, UK: 150 top right, 170 bottom
Roger Platts, UK: 151 top right
Nigel Dunnett, UK: 156 right, 161 bottom
Janine Crimmins, UK: 158
Robert Myers, UK: 160 top, 163 left
Nic Howard, UK: 163 top, 195 right, 197 left and top right
Jill Foxley, UK: 164 top
Greenes Garden Design, UK: 166 bottom right
LDC Design, UK: 168 right
Susan Willmott and Adele Ford, UK: 169 top and left
Jim Fogarty, Aust.: 169 bottom right, 173 top left
Joe Swift, UK: 171 bottom right
Nicole Fischer and Daniel Auderset, UK: 172 top right
CouCou Design, UK: 172 bottom right, 238
Thomas Hoblyn, UK: 179 top, 199 bottom right
Jack Dunckley, UK: 179 right
Acres Wild, UK: 180 bottom left
Claire Agnew, UK: 181 top
Hugo Bugg, UK: 181 bottom right
Jeni Cairns and Sophie Antonelli, UK: 182, 184 bottom and right, 185 top left, 188 top left
Brendan Moar, Aust.: 183, 187, 188 top right
Sean Murray, UK: 184 top left
Charlotte Murrell, UK: 185 third left
Rohan Thorn, Aust.: 189 top and middle
Tracy Foster, UK: 194 bottom right

John Mulvenna, UK: 196 bottom left and right
Jamie Durie, Aust.: 197 bottom right
Kate Ball, UK: 200
Caroline Comber, UK: 208 bottom
Matt Keighley, UK: 222

Locations
St James Court Hotel, London: 4, 5
Athenaeum Hotel, London: 8, 11, photographer Christian Trampenau
Moleshill House, UK: 65, 67, 94, 120 bottom right, 154 top right, bottom left, 180 top left
4 Ben's Acre, UK: 92, 105, 118 bottom, 127 top, 198 bottom,
Manor House Garden, UK: 100, 156 top left, 165 top left, 206 bottom right
Longleat Farm, Aust: 114
Wollerton Old Hall, UK: 124, 125 right, 175 top, 217 top left
The Old Croft, UK: 121 bottom left, 206 top left
Townland, UK: 126 bottom
Orchard House, UK: 127 bottom right
Chainhurst Cottage, UK: 128 top left, 178 top left, 219 top right
11 Raymer Road, UK: 128 top right, 129 bottom middle and right, 131 bottom left
Great Lywood Farmhouse, UK: 129 top
Rose Farm Studio, UK: 130 bottom right, 206 bottom middle, 206 bottom middle
Ringmer Park, UK: 131 top and bottom right
Church View, UK: 133
West Green Garden, UK: 134, 136, 212 middle right, 218 top right
Old Bladbean Stud, UK: 137 top left
Stonehealed, UK: 137 top right, 156 top right
Malthouse Farm, UK: 137 bottom left, 152 bottom, 153 top left, 156 bottom
Burnside, Aust: 137 bottom right, 212 bottom left
Godinton House, UK: 140 top and bottom right, 217 top right
Pashley Manor, UK: 141 bottom, sculptor Kate Denton
Lullingstone Castle, UK: 149 top right
Monksfield, UK: 149 bottom right
Charlotte Molesworth's garden, UK: 151 top left, 174 top
Melbourne Flower and Garden Show, Aust.: 135 top right, 151 bottom left, 157 top right, 162 top, bottom left, 164 bottom right, 167 top left and bottom, 171 top
Rose Farm Studio, UK: 152 top left, 172 top left, 216 bottom left
Driftwood, UK: 152 top right
Woodbury Cottage, UK: 171 bottom left
Timbers, UK: 174 bottom right
Dipley Mill, UK: 178 left middle, 185 top right
Sandhill Farm House, UK: 178 top right, 208 top left, 209 top, 210 top middle, 213 middle left, 217 bottom left
Wickham Lodge, UK: 201 top
Merriments, UK: 204, 209 bottom
Norton Court, UK: 205 bottom right, 210 bottom right
Lowder Mill, UK: 211 bottom right
Salutation, UK: 215 bottom left
Great Dixter, UK: 221 bottom right

LIVING WALL SUPPLIERS

UNITED KINGDOM:

ANS Global
Aldingbourne Nurseries,
Church Road,
Aldingbourne,
Chichester PO20 3TU
enquiries@ans.global

Atlantis Gro-Wall™
Unit 3
19-21 Gibbes Street
Chapswood
NSW 2067
Tel: 0294178344
info@atlantiscorp.com.au

Biotecture
The Old Dairy,
Ham Farm,
Main Road,
Bosham,
West Sussex, PO18 8EH
enquiries@biotecture.uk.com

Burgon and Ball
Vertiplant panels
Factory La Plata Works,
Holme Lane,
Sheffield, S6 4JY
enquiries@burgonandball.com

Fytogreen
Wrongs Farmhouse,
Wells Hall Road,
Great Cornard,
Sudbury, Suffolk CO10 0NH
info@fytogreen.uk.com

Landtech Soils Ltd UK.
Kao Hockham Building
Edinburgh Way
Harlow
Essex CM20 2NQ

info@landtechsoils.co.uk

Pixel-Garden Wall
Hy-Tex (UK) Limited
Aldington Mill
Mill Lane
Aldington
Ashford
Kent TN25 7AJ
sales@pixel-garden.co.uk

Scotscape
Ditton Nurseries,
Summerfield Lane,
Surbiton, Surrey, KT6 5DZ
sales@scotscape.net

Vertigarden
Ball Colegrave,
Milton Road,
West Adderbury,
Banbury,
Oxon, OX17 3EY
sales@vertigarden.co.uk

Vertology
Adjacent Manor Nursery,
Pagham Road,
Runcton,
Chichester,
West Sussex PO20 1LJ
hello@vertology.uk.com

UAE:

ANS Global
Plant Scapes
P.O. Box 37579,
Sheikh Zayed Road,
Dubai UAE
plantscapes@desertgroup.ae

Biotecture
Acacia LLC
PO Box: 126749, Dubai, UAE.
info@acacia-ae.com

USA:

Aerogation™ Wall Systems
AgroSci, Inc.
36dr Foote Road
Colchester, Ct. 06415
USA

sales@agrosci.com

Biotecture system
Sage Vertical Garden Systems,
730 West Randolph Street, Suite 300
Syracuse, N.Y.
information@sageall.com

Florafelt Vertical Garden Systems
6659 Peachtree Ind. Blvd., Suite B
Norcross, GA 30092 USA
info@plantsonwalls.com

Vertigarden
Vertical Garden Systems
2678 Reeves St. Dothan,
Alabama 36303
sales@verticalgardeningsystems.com

Woolly Pocket
901 E 14th Ave
North Kansas City, MO 64116
customerservice@woollypocket.com

NORWAY:

Biotecture
Bjørkmyr, 7036
Trondheim
Norway
 post@biowall.no

AUSTRALIA:

Fytogreen
3 Webbs Lane
Somerville VIC 3912
info@fytogreen.com.au

GreenWallAustralia
Bin Fen System
Wall Garden
Wallgarden.com.au
stephen@wallgarden.com.au

Vertical Gardens Australia
329 Ferrars St.,
South Melbourne, VIC 3205
enquiries@v-g-a.com.au

Vertigarden
Hightechort.com.au
dvanloon@bigpond.com

CANADA:

ELT Easy Green
245 King George Road,
Suite 320
 Brantford
Ontario N3R-7N7
info@elteasygreen.com
info@eltglobal.net

SINGAPORE:

Uniseal
119 Neo Tiew Ln,
Singapore 719098
info@uniseal.com.sg

First published in 2016 by New Holland Publishers Pty Ltd
London • Sydney • Auckland

The Chandlery Unit 704 50 Westminster Bridge Road London SE1 7QY United Kingdom
1/66 Gibbes Street Chatswood NSW 2067 Australia
5/39 Woodside Ave Northcote, Auckland 0627 New Zealand

www.newhollandpublishers.com

A record of this book is held at the British Library and the National Library of Australia.

ISBN: 9781742578798

Managing Director: Fiona Schultz
Publisher: Diane Ward
Project Editor: Jessica McNamara
Designer: Lorena Susak
Proofreader: Kate Lockley
Production Director: James Mills-Hicks
Printer: Times Printers

10 9 8 7 6 5 4 3 2 1

Keep up with New Holland Publishers on Facebook
www.facebook.com/NewHollandPublishers